LEGO NINJAGO®

CHARACTER ENCYCLOPEDIA
UPDATED AND EXPANDED

WRITTEN BY
SIMON HUGO AND CLAIRE SIPI

CONTENTS

NINJA VS. SKULKINS

5	Master Wu
6	Cole
7	Kai
8	Jay
9	Zane
10	Nya
11	Lord Garmadon
12	Samukai
13	Kruncha
14	Wyplash
15	Nuckal
16	Chopov
17	Skulkin Soldiers
18	Kai DX
19	Ninja DX

NINJA VS. SERPENTINE

21	Lloyd Garmadon
22	Cole ZX
23	Ninja ZX
24	Master Wu
25	Pythor P. Chumsworth
26	Acidicus
27	Venomari Tribe
28	Fangtom
29	Fangpyre Tribe
30	Skales
31	Hypnobrai Tribe
32	Skalidor
33	Constrictai Tribe
34	NRG Zane
35	NRG Ninja
36	Samurai X
37	Green Ninja

NINJA VS. OVERLORD

39	Kimono Kai
40	Kimono Jay
41	Kimono Cole
42	Kimono Zane
43	Golden Ninja
44	Lord Garmadon
45	Overlord
46	General Kozu
47	Stone Army Soldiers

NINJA VS. NINDROIDS

49	Master Garmadon
50	Cyrus Borg
51	Techno Cole
52	Techno Kai
53	Techno Ninja
54	Techno Wu
55	P.I.X.A.L.
56	General Cryptor
57	Nindroid Army

NINJA VS. ANACONDRAI CULT

59	Master Chen
60	Pythor
61	Skylor
62	Tournament Kai
63	Tournament Cole
64	Tournament Jay
65	Tournament Lloyd
66	Jungle Samurai X
67	Karlof
68	Griffin Turner
69	Elemental Masters
70	Titanium Zane
71	Clouse
72	Eyezor
73	Anacondrai Cult
74	Chope'rai
75	Kapau'rai
76	Jungle Kai
77	Jungle Ninja

NINJA VS. GHOST NINJA

79	Morro
80	Deepstone Lloyd
81	Evil Green Ninja
82	Deepstone Jay
83	Deepstone Kai
84	Deepstone Zane
85	Deepstone Cole
86	Ronin
87	Deepstone Nya
88	Soul Archer
89	Ghost Masters
90	Ming
91	Ghost Ninja
92	Airjitzu Kai
93	Airjitzu Ninja
94	Temple Wu
95	Misako
96	Ninjago Mailman
97	Dareth
98	Jesper
99	Claire

NINJA VS. SKY PIRATES

101	Nadakhan
102	Clancee
103	Flintlocke
104	Dogshank
105	Sky Pirate Crew
106	Destiny Jay
107	Destiny Nya
108	Ghost Cole
109	Destiny Ninja
110	Echo Zane
111	Tai-D

112 Prisoner Zane
113 Kryptarium Prison Crew
114 Master Yang
115 Yang's Student

NINJA VS. VERMILLION

117 General Machia
118 Acronix
119 Krux
120 Commander Blunck
121 Commander Raggmunk
122 Rivett
123 Vermillion Troops
124 Fusion Kai
125 Fusion Nya
126 Fusion Lloyd
127 Fusion Ninja
128 Ray
129 Maya

NINJA VS. SONS OF GARMADON

131 Resistance Lloyd
132 Snake Jaguar
133 P.I.X.A.L. Samurai X
134 Resistance Cole
135 Resistance Ninja
136 Princess Harumi
137 The Quiet One
138 Hutchins
139 Mr. E
140 Ultra Violet
141 Killow
142 Chopper Maroon
143 S.O.G. Gang Members
144 Hunted Skylor
145 Emperor Garmadon
146 Spinjitzu Master Kai
147 Spinjitzu Master Nya
148 Spinjitzu Master Jay
149 Spinjitzu Masters

NINJA VS. DRAGON HUNTERS

151 Hunted Lloyd
152 Hunted Nya
153 Hunted Ninja
154 Hunted Zane
155 Iron Baron
156 Heavy Metal
157 Daddy No Legs
158 Jet Jack
159 Dragon Hunters
160 Teen Wu
161 Dragon Master Wu
162 Dragon Master Jay
163 Dragon Masters

NINJA VS. FIRE AND ICE

165 Aspheera
166 Char
167 Pyro Vipers
168 Armor Kai
169 Armor Ninja
170 Armor Lloyd
171 Akita
172 Master Wu
173 Ice Emperor
174 General Vex
175 Blizzard Samurai
176 Nya FS
177 Jay FS
178 Cole FS
179 Ninja FS
180 Spinjitzu Slam Lloyd
181 Spinjitzu Slam Ninja

NINJA VS. GAME MASTER

183 Digi Jay
184 Digi Lloyd
185 Digi Ninja
186 Unagami
187 Red Visor
188 Avatar Jay

189 Avatar Lloyd
190 Avatar Pink Zane
191 Avatar Ninja
192 Okino
193 Scott
194 Avatar Harumi
195 NPCs

NINJA VS. SKULL SORCERER

197 Hero Cole
198 Hero Wu
199 Hero Zane
200 Hero Nya
201 Hero Ninja
202 Skull Sorcerer
203 Awakened Warrior
204 Murt
205 Gleck
206 Princess Vania
207 Spinjitzu Burst Ninja

NINJA VS. KEEPERS

209 Island Lloyd
210 Island Nya
211 Island Ninja
212 Island Jay
213 Chief Mammatus
214 PoulErik
215 Thunder Keeper
216 Rumble Keeper

NINJA CELEBRATION

218 Golden Legacy Kai
219 Golden Legacy Lloyd
220 Golden Legacy Ninja

222 Character Index
224 Acknowledgments

MASTER WU

SPINJITZU MASTER

NINJA FILE

LIKES: Drinking tea
DISLIKES: Siblings throwing tantrums
FRIENDS: New recruits
FOES: Lord Garmadon
SKILLS: Wisdom
GEAR: Bo staff

KEY SET: Monastery of Spinjitzu (Legacy)
SET NUMBER: 70670
YEAR: 2019

Master Wu's beard and mustache are removable

Magical writing protects Master Wu from dark powers

BROTHERLY BOTHER

Master Wu and his brother, Lord Garmadon, were trained by their father, the First Spinjitzu Master. He hoped that his sons would use their skills to protect the people of Ninjago Island. Lord Garmadon uses his powers selfishly, but Wu carries on his father's noble legacy.

MASTER WU IS THE SON of the First Spinjitzu Master, who created Ninjago Island. Wu has spent his life mastering the ancient martial art of Spinjitzu. He uses his skill and experience to guide a group of young ninja. He also protects Ninjago from his troublesome brother!

COLE
MASTER OF EARTH

Chain mail visible under robe (known as gi)

DID YOU KNOW?
Real-life ninja, medieval Japanese warriors, were trained from childhood in fighting, stealth, and survival.

Golden dragon emblem wraps around jacket

TEAM FIRST
Cole was the first student Master Wu recruited for ninja training. Cole enjoys focusing his energy and powers during Wu's grueling training routines. A spinning sword platform allows him to train alone or with his fellow ninja.

COLE IS AS STRONG and reliable as a rock. His natural strategic and leadership skills make him a key part of the ninja team. Cole always puts his team first and is a true friend to the other ninja. Cole can spin dirt and soil into a huge storm, reducing everything in its path to dust.

KAI
MASTER OF FIRE

Traditional headwrap made from two scarves to leave only the eyes uncovered

Sword of Fire is one of the four Golden Weapons

DID YOU KNOW?

Kai's father guarded a map that showed the location of the four Golden Weapons used to create the Realm of Ninjago.

Sashes and belts are an essential part of a ninja's outfit

NINJA FILE

LIKES: Rushing into danger
DISLIKES: Losing battles
FRIENDS: Master Wu and Nya
FOES: Samukai, Frakjaw
SKILLS: Making weapons
GEAR: Sword of Fire

KEY SET: Monastery of Spinjitzu (Legacy)
SET NUMBER: 70670
YEAR: 2019

FAMILY HISTORY
Kai and his sister, Nya, took over the family Blacksmith Shop (set 2508) when their parents disappeared. Wu saw that Kai had the potential to be a ninja and trained him to use his natural "fire" to master Spinjitzu.

THIS NINJA'S ELEMENT is fire, and his temper is equally hot! Kai accepts Master Wu's challenge to train as a ninja, but he must work hard to control his anger and impatience. Master Wu's faith in Kai is justified—he soon becomes a brave, loyal, and skillful ninja. He channels his fiery energy into Spinjitzu.

JAY
MASTER OF LIGHTNING

NINJA FILE

LIKES: Witty jokes
DISLIKES: Broken technology
FRIENDS: Nya
FOES: Nuckal, Krazi
SKILLS: Inventing
GEAR: Nunchucks of Lightning

KEY SET: Monastery of Spinjitzu (Legacy)
SET NUMBER: 70670
YEAR: 2019

Nunchucks of Lightning have dragon-head handles

Gi design matches nunchuck handles

LIGHTNING SPINJITZU
Jay was the first of the ninja to master the art of Spinjitzu. Now, as quick as a flash, he can spin to turn into a lightning tornado crackling with electric ninja energy.

LIGHTNING IS HIS ELEMENT, and Jay is lightning-fast in combat. His flair for crazy inventions, his thirst for adventure, and his sense of humor are just some of the qualities that Master Wu knew would make Jay a good, skillful ninja. Jay is also creative and loves solving problems.

ZANE

MASTER OF ICE

DID YOU KNOW?

When he became a ninja, Zane looked completely human and did not realize that he was actually a robot, or Nindroid (ninja-droid).

Zane's artificial eyes are an icy blue

Two Shurikens of Ice make up one of the Golden Weapons

Black hands contrast with Zane's white robes but are featured on all the ninja recruits

NINJA FILE

LIKES: Cooking
DISLIKES: Jokes
FRIENDS: Master Wu
FOES: Wyplash, Bonezai
SKILLS: Logic
GEAR: Shurikens of Ice

KEY SET: Monastery of Spinjitzu (Legacy)
SET NUMBER: 70670
YEAR: 2019

NINJA GLIDER

The ninja first appeared in LEGO® sets in 2011 in simple training robes. In Ninja Glider (set 30080), the original Zane minifigure has a glider made from six golden blades and carries an additional black katana.

ZANE IS QUIET, serious, and focused. He learns quickly and is curious about everything. Zane watches and waits for the right moment to strike. He is so quiet and stealthy that he can creep up on his enemies without being detected. However, his friends' jokes often pass him by undetected in return!

NYA
THE WATER NINJA

Nya can use many different weapons, including daggers

Robes with phoenix detail are printed on legs

NINJA FILE

LIKES: Her independence
DISLIKES: Being kidnapped
FRIENDS: Jay
FOES: Skulkin
SKILLS: Tech wiz
GEAR: Daggers, staff

KEY SET: Fire Temple
SET NUMBER: 2507
YEAR: 2011

DID YOU KNOW?

Nya was the first LEGO® NINJAGO® minifigure to have a double-sided head. She was followed by Lloyd, P.I.X.A.L., and many others.

FLOWING HER OWN WAY

Nya forged her own path before becoming the Water Ninja in 2015. In the 2019 Legacy set Monastery of Spinjitzu (set 70670), Nya appears in full ninja training garb, alongside the four original ninja and Lloyd.

NYA IS KAI'S SISTER. She works with Kai in the Four Weapons Blacksmith Shop. Although she doesn't become a ninja immediately, tough Nya is every bit as capable as her brother. She trains hard and is always ready to battle evil. Nya uses her skills with computers to spy on the ninja's enemies.

LORD GARMADON

KING OF SHADOWS

Underworld helmet helps to control the Skulkins

Thunder Bolt weapon can zap foes with electricity

FOUR-ARMED FOE

Garmadon becomes a regular foe of the ninja. As his powers grow, he grows taller and even gets an extra set of arms! His four-armed form appears in many sets, including 2019's The Ultra Dragon (Legacy set 70679.)

Extra arms allow Garmadon to wield four weapons at once

MASTER WU'S BROTHER, Lord Garmadon, was infected with a powerful, villainous energy long ago. He was banished to the Underworld, but is now on a quest to defeat his brother and destroy Ninjago Island. He trains his bony Skulkin followers in the ways of Spinjitzu, making them fearsome foes.

Unique skull markings

Pivoting head piece allows mouth to open

NINJA FILE

LIKES: Being in charge
DISLIKES: Following orders
FRIENDS: Fellow generals
FOES: Lord Garmadon
SKILLS: Plotting schemes
GEAR: Nunchucks, shurikens, scythe

KEY SET: Garmadon's Dark Fortress
SET NUMBER: 2505
YEAR: 2011

MEETING THEIR MATCH

The ninja are still in training when they must defend Ninjago against the Skulkin forces. Kai puts his fiery Spinjitzu powers to the test against Samukai—it is blaze versus blades!

Four bony arms allow Samukai to wield multiple weapons at once

ONCE THE KING of the Underworld, Samukai's reign was overthrown by Lord Garmadon. Now, the fearsome Samukai leads the Skulkins into battle against the ninja, under Garmadon's control. Garmadon plans to use four-armed Samukai to wield the four Golden Weapons.

KRUNCHA
HARD-HATTED GENERAL

Accessories can be clipped onto helmet

NINJA FILE

LIKES: Being proved right
DISLIKES: Being ignored
FRIENDS: Obedient soldiers
FOES: Pesky ninja
SKILLS: Bellowing orders
GEAR: Dark blade

KEY SET: The Samurai Mech (Legacy)
SET NUMBER: 70665
YEAR: 2019

BODY ARMOR
In 2011 sets such as Lightning Dragon Battle (set 2521), Kruncha wears a monocle over his right eye. His head and helmet are one unique piece, and his large, printed shoulder armor is also exclusive to him.

Jagged blade is heavy and sharp

Loincloth printed on standard skeleton torso

LOUD, HARD, AND STRONG, Kruncha is one of the four generals who leads the Skulkins. Kruncha takes everything seriously and expects others to do the same. He often shouts at his minions but is also constantly bickering with his fellow general, Nuckal.

WYPLASH
SUSPICIOUS SKULKIN

Same hat as Master Wu

Dagger is small but sharp

NINJA FILE

LIKES: Keeping watch
DISLIKES: Not knowing what is going on
FRIENDS: He trusts no one
FOES: Watchful Nya
SKILLS: Stealth
GEAR: Dagger

KEY SET: Monastery of Spinjitzu (Legacy)
SET NUMBER: 70670
YEAR: 2019

SKULL DECORATION
Back in 2011, Wyplash looked a little different. In sets such as Earth Dragon Defense (set 2521), he wears the same hat but on top of a larger skull, complete with a worm crawling out of one side!

Worm could be the cause of Wyplash's headaches

WYPLASH IS A SKULKIN GENERAL and Samukai's second-in-command. Stealth is his special skill, and he always watches and waits for the right moment to attack his enemy. Paranoid Wyplash can turn his huge skull backward, which means he can always see the enemy approaching.

NUCKAL

HAIR-RAISING VILLAIN

Mohawk hair piece plugs into skull

Metal eye patch

NINJA FILE

LIKES: Causing mayhem
DISLIKES: Being bored
FRIENDS: Krazi and other mischievous Skulkins
FOES: Anyone in his way
SKILLS: Bravery
GEAR: Iron bone ax

KEY SET: The Samurai Mech (Legacy)
SET NUMBER: 70665
YEAR: 2019

HISTORIC HAIR

Nuckal first appeared in three 2011 sets, with skull spikes that were more like dinosaur ridges than a hairstyle! In Spinjitzu Dojo (set 2504), he carries a silver dark blade, as well as an ax.

DID YOU KNOW?

Nuckal has unusual arm pieces in the spinner set Nuckal (set 2173). They allow him to hold weapons horizontally.

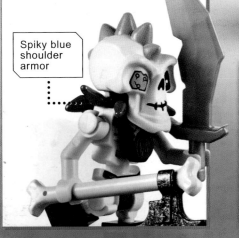

Spiky blue shoulder armor

NUCKAL IS CHILDISH, wild, and very dangerous. He loves fighting, and if there is trouble to be found, Nuckal will find it! This bony brute's idea of fun is striking ninja down with his quick reflexes. Nuckal's battle moves are often combined with a cackling and electrifying laugh.

CHOPOV
SKULKIN MECHANIC

Black metal helmet

Bone ax

Black boots worn by all 2011 Skulkins

NINJA FILE

LIKES: Dreaming big
DISLIKES: Flat tires
FRIENDS: Other Skulkin warriors
FOES: Earth Ninja Cole
SKILLS: Engineering
GEAR: Bronzed bone ax

KEY SET: Skull Motorbike
SET NUMBER: 2259
YEAR: 2011

SKULL MOTORBIKE

Chopov's battle vehicle from set 2259 is a cool chopper motorbike. He uses it in battle or for quick escapes. The powerful skull hammerhead can smash anything in its path, especially ninja!

Catapult hinge mechanism

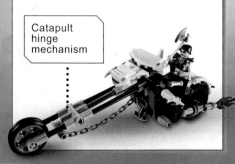

CHOPOV IS VERY TOUGH. He does not let anything get in his way, even ninja! This smart warrior is also the chief mechanic of the Skulkins and maintains all of the vehicles. Chopov secretly wishes that he, instead of Bonezai, could get creative and also design the Skulkins' super-cool vehicles.

SKULKIN SOLDIERS
BONEHEADED BAD GUYS

Don't let his smile fool you—Bonezai is a true threat!

Battle-scarred torso printing

NINJA FILE

NAME: Bonezai
KEY SET: Ninja Ambush
SET NUMBER: 2258
YEAR: 2011

NINJA FILE

NAME: Krazi
KEY SET: Ice Dragon Attack
SET NUMBER: 2260
YEAR: 2011

Removable jester's hat in red and blue

NINJA FILE

NAME: Frakjaw
KEY SET: Lightning Dragon Battle
SET NUMBER: 2521
YEAR: 2011

Helmet with goggles protects Frakjaw in battle

Stolen Shuriken of Ice

Golden mace increases Frakjaw's attack range when he launches into his Spinjitzu moves

THESE LOW-RANKING Skulkin warriors might not be in charge, but they all have special talents. Krazi wears a jester's hat and clown makeup to confuse his enemy, while talkative Frakjaw uses chatter as a distraction. Bonezai uses his skills to design vehicles for the Skulkins.

KAI DX

FIRE DRAGON EXTREME

NINJA FILE

LIKES: Flying fast on Flame

DISLIKES: Losing dragon races

FRIENDS: Flame

FOES: The Skulkins

SKILLS: Dragon-whispering

GEAR: Black katana, Sword of Fire

KEY SET: Fire Temple

SET NUMBER: 2507

YEAR: 2011

Kai's hood is the same as his orignal 2011 training uniform

Golden Fire Dragon printed on robe breathes the element of fire

ELEMENTAL BOND

Kai bonds with this mighty Fire Dragon. The creature is guardian of the Fire Temple. Kai names him Flame—a fitting name for a creature who is red-hot from nose to tail!

Fiery head contains weapons launcher inside the jaws

Kai uses a normal katana before mastering his Golden Weapon

KAI MANAGES TO TAME his dragon and gains DX (Dragon eXtreme) ranking and a new ninja dragon costume to match. Kai first enlists the help of his dragon when the ninja need to travel to the Underworld. Kai is able to encourage his dragon to use its incredible speed to fly to Master Wu's aid.

NINJA DX
DRAGON EXTREME ROBES

Distinctive eyebrows give Jay's identity away

NINJA FILE

NAME: Zane DX
KEY SET: Ice Dragon Attack
SET NUMBER: 2260
YEAR: 2011

Removable hood disguises Zane's face

NINJA FILE

NAME: Jay DX
KEY SET: Lightning Dragon Battle
SET NUMBER: 2521
YEAR: 2011

New dark blue obi sash

Ice Dragon breathes out freezing blasts of ice

DID YOU KNOW?

All the DX ninja have back printing. Each ninja has their name and elemental symbol on the back of their robes.

NINJA FILE

NAME: Cole DX
KEY SET: Earth Dragon Defense
SET NUMBER: 2509
YEAR: 2011

Scythe of Quakes is linked to the Earth element

EACH NINJA TAMES their dragon differently. Clever Jay invents a dragon-roar amplifier to befriend Wisp, the Lightning Dragon, but poor Zane initially gets frozen solid by Shard, the Ice Dragon. Cole has to overcome his fear of dragons to bond with the Earth Dragon, who he names Rocky.

Earth Dragon's huge scaly tail is printed on both legs

SSSEEMSSS LIKE A SSSTORY I COULD SSSINK MY TEETH INTO!

CHAPTER TWO

NINJA VS. SERPENTINE

THE SECOND THREAT the ninja face comes from the snakelike Serpentine tribes. If the ninja are to stop the serpents from taking over Ninjago Island, they must unlock their True Potential and add a new, green member to their team!

LLOYD GARMADON
SON OF LORD GARMADON

NINJA FILE

LIKES: Causing trouble
DISLIKES: Being left out
FRIENDS: Serpentine
FOES: The ninja
SKILLS: Annoying everyone nearby
GEAR: Small dagger

KEY SET: Destiny's Bounty (Legacy)
SET NUMBER: 71705
YEAR: 2020

Black-hooded cloak is removable

TWO-FACED
Having the most evil father in all the land is a difficult legacy for Lloyd to live up to. He switches between playing annoying pranks and being scared of his father's powers—as his face reflects!

Torso printing designed to look like Lord Garmadon's chest

Green "5" hints at Lloyd's future as the fifth ninja

LLOYD GARMADON is not as bad as his father, Lord Garmadon. He attends Darkley's Boarding School for Bad Boys and is more interested in candy and practical jokes than plotting to take over Ninjago Island. Young Lloyd accidentally releases the Serpentine tribes and becomes their unlikely leader.

COLE ZX
EARTH ZEN EXTREME

Pauldrons do not feature on every variant of Cole ZX

This three-pronged weapon is the ultimate Serpentine repellent

Protective leather-style chest plate

NINJA FILE

LIKES: The open road
DISLIKES: Punctures
FRIENDS: Zane
FOES: Lasha and all snakes
SKILLS: Driving his Tread Assault vehicle
GEAR: Golden sai blades

KEY SET: Cole's Tread Assault
SET NUMBER: 9444
YEAR: 2012

DID YOU KNOW?
The Serpentine can be controlled by sacred flute music. The ninja play recordings of this music as a secret weapon.

TOTAL TREAD ASSAULT
Cole's Tread Assault vehicle first appears to be a typical tank with oversized wheels, in Cole's traditional black. Underneath the main body, however, lies green camouflage that allows it to sneak up on unsuspecting snakes!

THANKS TO HOURS of practice, Cole has achieved the ZX, or Zen, level of his ninja training. To mark his new status, Cole wears silver pauldrons to protect his upper body. As leader of the ninja, it is now Cole's job to help the others develop their own Zen eXtreme skills.

New robes feature one arm covered in protective silver armor

Removable ZX hood with new gold crown detail

NINJA FILE

NAME: Kai ZX
KEY SET: Kai's Blade Cycle
SET NUMBER: 9441
YEAR: 2012

Pauldron piece has a slot at the back that can hold two katana blades

Protective chest plate worn over red tunic

NINJA FILE

NAME: Jay ZX
KEY SET: Epic Dragon Battle
SET NUMBER: 9450
YEAR: 2012

NINJA FILE

NAME: Zane ZX
KEY SET: Fangpyre Truck Ambush
SET NUMBER: 9445
YEAR: 2012

In Hidden Sword (set 30086), a variant of this minifigure appears without golden armor

Zane's new robes feature entwined rope belts

WITH COLE'S HELP, the other ninja soon achieve Zen eXtreme level. The ninja's new robes show off their new ZX status. The belts, buckles, and other robe details are different for each ninja, but they have all upgraded their old armor and head pieces for shiny metallic versions!

MASTER WU
CAPTAIN OF DESTINY'S BOUNTY

NINJA FILE

LIKES: Meditating
DISLIKES: Being disturbed
FRIENDS: Reformed
brother Garmadon
FOES: Serpentine
SKILLS: Mastery of
Elements and Spinjitzu
GEAR: Bo staff

KEY SET: Destiny's Bounty
SET NUMBER: 9446
YEAR: 2012

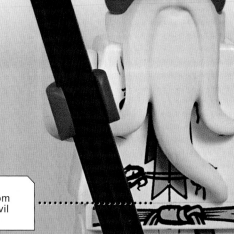

An otherwise identical Wu wears a shinier hat in Epic Dragon Battle (set 9450) and Temple of Light (set 70505)

Snake symbols on robe protect Wu from evil, snakes, and evil snakes!

The hem of Wu's robe is printed on his legs

MARK OF A MASTER
A version of Wu with less detailed robes appears in three 2011 sets, including Spinjitzu Dojo (set 2504). His black belt indicates that he has reached the level of expert in at least one martial art—and probably many others!

CALM AND SELF-DISCIPLINED Master Wu is the perfect teacher. He uses knowledge from years of training to guide the ninja to reach the next three levels—ZX (Zen eXtreme), Kendo, and NRG. In the flying ship *Destiny's Bounty*, he searches for a new ninja base. Luckily, he doesn't get sea- or airsick!

PYTHOR P. CHUMSWORTH

LAST OF THE ANACONDRAI

NINJA FILE

LIKES: Evil schemes
DISLIKES: Getting his hands dirty
FRIENDS: Serpentine minions
FOES: Everyone!
SKILLS: Evil mastermind
GEAR: Serpentine staff, Fang Blades

KEY SET: Jay's Storm Fighter (Legacy)
SET NUMBER: 70668
YEAR: 2019

Long necks are the Anacondrai's most distinctive feature

DID YOU KNOW?
While imprisoned, the Anacondrai started eating each other! Pythor ended up a general with no followers but a full stomach!

Winding snake-tail part first created for Anacondrai characters in 2012

Open-mouthed head with fangs for eating friends and foes alike!

NEVER TRUST A SNAKE
When Pythor finally gets his hands on all four Fang Blades, he uses them to release the Great Devourer. His moment of triumph is short-lived—the first thing the Great Devourer does is devour Pythor!

PYTHOR WAS GENERAL of the Anacondrai, the most feared snake tribe around. After their imprisonment many years ago, he is now the tribe's last surviving member. Pythor wants all four Fang Blades so that he can release the Great Devourer and destroy Ninjago Island.

ACIDICUS

VENOMARI GENERAL

DID YOU KNOW?

The Venomari tribe's toxic venom causes terrible hallucinations in its victims. Acidicus keeps a vial of anti-venom in a special staff.

NINJA FILE

LIKES: Devious weapons
DISLIKES: Venom shortages
FRIENDS: Other generals
FOES: Skalidor, at times
SKILLS: Inventive mind
GEAR: Venomari Fang Blade

KEY SET: Epic Dragon Battle
SET NUMBER: 9450
YEAR: 2012

Acidicus has two side fangs, as well as two front fangs

All Serpent Generals have a snake tail instead of legs

ONE OF FOUR

There are four ancient silver Fang Blades, one for each of the four large tribes. Each blade is filled with the venom of its tribe. The Venomari blade has a gruesome green vial of venom at its base.

GENERAL OF THE Venomari, Acidicus is very crafty. He has constructed special vials that the Venomari use to carry extra venom in their combat gear, so they never run out of poison in battle. How brilliantly evil! However, no one knows where clever Acidicus keeps his own vials—maybe there are pockets in his tail!

VENOMARI TRIBE

VIAL VILLAINS

Fangs are too large for Spitta's mouth, so he is always dribbling venom!

Long Serpentine scythe contains a vial of venom

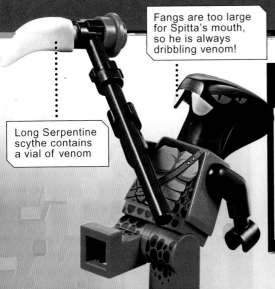

Distinctive striped head markings

NINJA FILE

NAME: Spitta
KEY SET: Kai's Blade Cycle & Zane's Snowmobile (Legacy)
SET NUMBER: 70667
YEAR: 2019

Scaly, scarred torso similar to other members of the Venomari tribe

NINJA FILE

NAME: Lasha
KEY SET: Kai's Blade Cycle & Zane's Snowmobile (Legacy)
SET NUMBER: 70667
YEAR: 2019

Missing eye doesn't stop Lasha from being the tribe's best scout

NINJA FILE

NAME: Lizaru
KEY SET: Lizaru
SET NUMBER: 9557
YEAR: 2012

THE VENOMARI TRIBE are truly toxic! This group of swamp-dwelling Serpentine use vials of their naturally occuring venom to poison their enemies. Head shape and size gives an important clue to a Serpent's rank in their tribe, from second-in-command Lizaru, down to junior scout Lasha.

Bandolier shoulder belt to hold vials

Two small heads sprouting from original neck

NINJA FILE

LIKES: Thinking out elaborate strategies
DISLIKES: Disorder
FRIENDS: Skales
FOES: Master Wu
SKILLS: Strong leadership
GEAR: Golden Fangpyre Staff

KEY SET: Fangpyre Truck Ambush
SET NUMBER: 9445
YEAR: 2012

Like all the Serpent Generals, Fangtom has a tail instead of legs

CAN'T GET THE STAFF

As General of the Fangpyre tribe, Fangtom carries the Golden Fangpyre Staff. A vial of anti-venom tailored to the Fangpyre's unique poison is held in the staff, and its end is twisted like a serpent's tail.

FANGTOM IS THE Fangpyre tribe's general. He accidentally bit himself when he was trying to turn one of his victims into a snake, and his poison caused his head to form two smaller heads. Two heads are definitely better than one for Fangtom. He is the brains of the tribe and can cause double the trouble for the ninja!

FANGPYRE TRIBE

SNAKE-MAKING SNAKES

NINJA FILE

NAME: Fangdam
KEY SET: Fangpyre Truck Ambush
SET NUMBER: 9445
YEAR: 2012

Double-headed head piece is identical to that of his brother, Fangtom

Snappa wears a similar fanged necklace to Fang-Suei, but with fewer teeth attached

Fangpyre scale pattern continues onto legs

Distinctive narrow head and long neck is the same mold as that used for Constrictai Chokun, but here in Fangpyre colors

Unique necklace made of fangs

DID YOU KNOW?

Fangdam grew his second head after fellow Serpent Fang-Suei mistook him for a desert slug and bit him!

NINJA FILE

NAME: Snappa
KEY SET: Jay's Storm Fighter
SET NUMBER: 9442
YEAR: 2012

NINJA FILE

NAME: Fang-Suei
KEY SET: Fangpyre Mech
SET NUMBER: 9455
YEAR: 2012

RED IS A WARNING SIGN, so watch out for the bright-red markings of the Fangpyre tribe! A poisonous bite from a Fangpyre can turn anything or anyone into a snake. Always hungry, Fang-Suei bites anything he can find. He turns many machines into snakelike vehicles for his tribe.

29

SKALES

HYPNOBRAI GENERAL

Blue cobralike hood with hypnotic pattern

NINJA FILE

LIKES: Seizing control
DISLIKES: Incompetent leaders
FRIENDS: Fangpyre General Fangtom
FOES: Slithraa, ninja
SKILLS: Fang-Kwon-Do
GEAR: Pike, Golden Staff

KEY SET: Cole's Tread Assualt
SET NUMBER: 9444
YEAR: 2012

Battle pike can grab and snap other weapons

DID YOU KNOW?

There is no love lost between the Serpentine tribes, but at one time, the Hypnobrai and Fangpyre tribes were allies.

HYPNOTIC!

Now that he is General of the Hypnobrai Tribe, Skales looks after the Hypnobrai Golden Staff. As the Hypnobrai have powerful, hypnotic eyes, this Staff contains the anti-venom to reverse a hypnotic trance.

THIS COLD AND CALCULATING snake became leader of the Hypnobrai tribe when he beat General Slithraa in a fight. Skales is one of the toughest Serpents around and is always looking for opportunities to fulfill his ambitions for control and power. He is skilled in Fang-Kwon-Do, an ancient martial art.

HYPNOBRAI TRIBE

DON'T LOOK THEM IN THE EYE!

NINJA FILE

NAME: Mezmo
KEY SET: Mezmo
SET NUMBER: 9555
YEAR: 2012

Two large fangs overhang Mezmo's mouth

Swirling blue and yellow Hypnobrai patterns decorate torso, head, and legs

Blue, yellow, and gray coloring matches the other members of his tribe

Slithraa lost his tail and regrew legs when Skales took over the position of General

Each of the Hypnobrai have unique markings beginning at the very top of their heads

NINJA FILE

NAME: Rattla
KEY SET: Kai's Blade Cycle
SET NUMBER: 9441
YEAR: 2012

NINJA FILE

NAME: Slithraa
KEY SET: Destiny's Bounty
SET NUMBER: 9446
YEAR: 2012

Powerful red-eyed hypnotic stare

THE HYPNOBRAI TRIBE were sealed away in the snowy mountains until Lloyd Garmadon accidentally released them. This cobralike tribe have hypnotic powers. With one look of their swirling red eyes, Hypnobrai warriors can force their enemies into doing whatever they want.

SKALIDOR

CONSTRICTAI GENERAL

The general has a distinctive head piece with silver spikes

DID YOU KNOW?
The Constrictai Serpents live underground in caves and tunnels. When they move above ground, they are so heavy that they make cracks in the earth.

This weapon is multifunctional—pairing a sharp spear with a double-headed ax

BATTLE HUNGRY

Alongside General Acidicus of the Venomari tribe, Skalidor leads the Serpentine forces and the Great Devourer in an epic battle against the ninja and the Ultra Dragon. The snakes want to devour all of Ninjago Island in their hungry jaws!

PLUMP BUT POWERFUL Skalidor is General of the Constrictai tribe. He isn't quite as athletic as the rest of his tribe, but he can can crush his enemies with a single blow or even with the weight of his body. Ninja, don't be fooled by his size—Skalidor's reflexes are fast!

CONSTRICTAI TRIBE
THEY'RE CRUSHING IT!

Bytar's head piece is similar to General Skalidor's but features bright orange spikes

Separate head piece with boa attachment slots on top of minifigure head

Scout Snike has the simplest head design due to his low rank

NINJA FILE

NAME: Bytar
KEY SET: Samurai Mech
SET NUMBER: 9448
YEAR: 2012

Sinister, narrow head with gray and white scales

All the Constrictai warriors have short legs

Constrictai soldier Chokun wields a golden mace

DID YOU KNOW?

Constrictai soldiers and scouts have similar orange torsos but unique gray scale markings.

NINJA FILE

NAME: Snike
KEY SET: Samurai Mech
SET NUMBER: 9448
YEAR: 2012

NINJA FILE

NAME: Chokun
KEY SET: Epic Dragon Battle
SET NUMBER: 9450
YEAR: 2012

THE SHORTEST TRIBE in the Serpentine Army is also the strongest. The Constrictai use their viselike grips to crush their enemies. These muscular snakes are also as stealthy as ninja, lurking in their underground hideouts until they are ready to strike.

NRG ZANE

ICY BLAST

NINJA FILE

LIKES: Icy cold colors
DISLIKES: The color pink
FRIENDS: NRG ninja
FOES: His own memories
SKILLS: Complete mastery of ice
GEAR: Elemental power

KEY SET: NRG Zane
SET NUMBER: 9590
YEAR: 2012

DID YOU KNOW?

Each of the ninja achieves their "True Potential" by accepting an important truth about who they really are.

Sharp, jagged burst on Zane's chest resembles a powerful blast of ice energy

Zane is the only NRG ninja to have hands in a different color from his arms

SECRET PAST

Zane is overwhelmed when learns that he is a Nindroid, built from scratch by the brilliant Dr. Julien. Activating a switch in his circuitry restores many happy memories of his genius "father."

DESPITE ALL THE OBSTACLES standing in his way, Zane is the first of the ninja team to reach his True Potential. For him, this means finding out that he is a robot rather than flesh and blood. When he accepts the truth about who he is, Zane becomes more determined than ever to stop his Serpentine foes.

NRG NINJA
REACHING THEIR TRUE POTENTIAL

NINJA FILE

NAME: NRG Kai
KEY SET: Weapon Pack
SET NUMBER: 9591
YEAR: 2012

A red-hot fireball fittingly decorates Kai's NRG robes

DID YOU KNOW?
Each of the NRG ninja variants appears in one set only, making their True Potential level a rare find!

Ninja hood is decorated with lightning-bolt burst

Sparks and flames extend to Kai's legs

Lightning energy crackles around Jay's eyes

Earth emblem appears in vibrant colors on Cole's new robes

NINJA FILE

NAME: NRG Jay
KEY SET: NRG Jay
SET NUMBER: 9570
YEAR: 2012

Cole's favorite color is actually orange, but his new NRG robes are instead decorated pink

NINJA FILE

NAME: NRG Cole
KEY SET: NRG Cole
SET NUMBER: 9572
YEAR: 2012

EACH NINJA FACES a different challenge to unlock their True Potential. Jay confronts his romantic feelings for Nya, while Cole resolves his rocky relationship with his father. Kai has to look inside himself and learn to control his fiery temper. All of the ninja succeed, reach NRG level, and are rewarded with some explosively colorful new robes.

NINJA FILE

LIKES: Sword practice
DISLIKES: Being told to stay away from fighting, not being taken seriously
FRIENDS: Jay
FOES: Serpentine
SKILLS: Building robots
GEAR: Giant mech sword, katana swords

KEY SET: The Samurai Mech (Legacy)
SET NUMBER: 70665
YEAR: 2019

Ornamental spiked Samurai crest tops protective helmet

Protective body armor covers red warrior dress robes and comes with extended shoulder pads

Twin katanas double as talons on Nya's Samurai Mech

ARMED FOR BATTLE
The Samurai X variant in 2014's Battle for Ninjago City (set 70728) has intricate printed armor instead of a chest plate accessory. Her silver shoulder armor piece has room to store two crossed katana swords.

Red mask hides Nya's face and true identity

DID YOU KNOW?
Smart Nya is able to cure a Fangpyre bite and knows that getting just one Fang Blade will stop the Great Devourer!

WHO IS HIDDEN behind Samurai X's mask? For a while, no one knows who this warrior is, but one day the truth is revealed. Samurai X is Nya, Kai's sister! Nya has trained by herself and developed warrior skills as impressive as those of the ninja. She's also built herself impressive armor and a mech battle suit!

GREEN NINJA
MASTER OF ENERGY

NINJA FILE

LIKES: Becoming a hero
DISLIKES: Fighting his father
FRIENDS: The ninja
FOES: Forces of evil!
SKILLS: Wielding the powers of the four elements
GEAR: Golden katanas

KEY SET: The Ultra Dragon (Legacy)
SET NUMBER: 70679
YEAR: 2019

Green eyes for a Green Ninja!

Shape of toes shows through fabric footwear

Dragon design decorates simple green gi

DID YOU KNOW?
A magical tea caused young Lloyd to grow older, making him the same age as the other ninja. His minifigure legs grew, too!

KIMONO KEEPSAKE
A variant of the Green Ninja was available exclusively in the original DK LEGO® NINJAGO® *Character Encyclopedia*. This minifigure has an elaborate, green-and-gold kimono, possibly hinting at a golden future for Lloyd.

AN ANCIENT PROPHECY foretold that a Green Ninja would rise above all others to fight the darkness. Surprisingly, the Green Ninja's identity is revealed to be none other than Lloyd Garmadon. The transformative powers of the Golden Weapons turn him into the Green Ninja.

BAD LUCK COMES IN THREES for the ninja, as a trio of dangers combine into one! A Stone Army rises from underground; Lord Garmadon returns; and the ancient being known as the Overlord makes both threats more menacing than ever!

THIS CHAPTER IS A STONE-COLD CLASSIC!

CHAPTER THREE

NINJA VS. OVERLORD

KIMONO KAI
ELEMENTAL FIRE NINJA

NINJA FILE

LIKES: His Fire Mech
DISLIKES: Fighting evil Nya
FRIENDS: Kimono ninja
FOES: Greedy Overlords
SKILLS: Fighting off
Garmadon's scouts
GEAR: Elemental
Fire Blade

KEY SET: Kai's Fire Mech
SET NUMBER: 70500
YEAR: 2013

MAJOR FIREPOWER!
The awesome Fire Mech's huge robot form has impenetrable armor, cannons, katana swords, and serrated blades. Kai pilots it from a cockpit at the top.

Warrior headwrap with gold three-point crown visor

DID YOU KNOW?
This version of Kai, wearing his elemental robes, is quite rare, as it can only be found in Kai's Fire Mech (set 70500).

Elemental kimono with sash complete with fire symbol on the back

Double-edged elemental Blade of Fire

IN THE TEMPLE OF LIGHT, fiery Kai gets his elemental powers back, and his new kimono-style robe reflects the powerful energy now coursing through him. Red-hot Kai is ready to fight the Overlord's Stone Warriors in his mighty Fire Mech, in a titanic battle for control of the four elemental blades.

KIMONO JAY
ELEMENTAL LIGHTNING NINJA

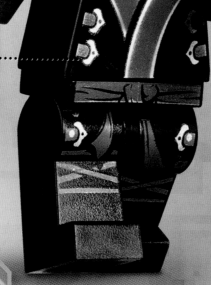

NINJA FILE

LIKES: Fiery rocket pack
DISLIKES: Fast missiles
FRIENDS: Kimono ninja
FOES: General Kozu
SKILLS: Escaping the Stone Warriors' Warrior Bike
GEAR: Elemental Lightning Blade

KEY SET: Warrior Bike
SET NUMBER: 70501
YEAR: 2013

Elemental kimono with sash and lightning symbol on the back

Elemental Lightning Blade

TEMPLE OF LIGHT TRANSFORMATION

When Lloyd strikes the bell in the Temple of Light, the energy produced raises the ninja to a higher elemental status. Jay regains his power over lightning, and his sword manifests a blade representing this element.

DID YOU KNOW?

Jay uses a jet pack to escape from the Stone Warrior, who is in hot pursuit on his Warrior Bike (set 70501).

JAY LEADS THE NINJA to the Temple of Light, where he undergoes his transformation and wears a striking new elemental kimono to reflect his elevated status. He is once again master of his element and will need his fast reflexes to protect the elemental Lightning Blade.

KIMONO COLE
ELEMENTAL EARTH NINJA

NINJA FILE

LIKES: Defeating the
Stone Warriors
DISLIKES: Losing his
elemental Earth Blade
FRIENDS: Kimono ninja
FOES: Stone Swordsman
SKILLS: Drilling
GEAR: Elemental
Earth Blade

KEY SET: Cole's
Earth Driller
SET NUMBER: 70502
YEAR: 2013

Ninja headwrap
protects Cole's
identity

Kimono in Cole's
trademark black
with gray detail

COLE'S EARTH DRILLER
This super-tough armored vehicle
has a powerful rotating drill piece
and can plow its way through any
obstacle—including stone! With
Cole in the driver's seat, the ninja
use these wheels to escape from
the Stone Warriors.

Spinning
drill piece

AFTER HAVING LOST but then regained
his powers, Cole can't wait to take charge
and see off the Stone Warriors. His sleek
new kimono-style outfit is perfect for the job.
Wielding the Earth Blade and harnessing
his element, Cole is a force to be reckoned
with. He has never been stronger.

KIMONO ZANE
ELEMENTAL ICE NINJA

NINJA FILE

LIKES: New robes
DISLIKES: Island of Darkness
FRIENDS: Dr. Julien
FOES: General Kozu
SKILLS: Firing freezing bolts from Ice Spider Mech
GEAR: Elemental Ice Blade

KEY SET: Garmatron
SET NUMBER: 70504
YEAR: 2013

Elemental kimono with sash and ice symbol on the back

Elemental Ice Blade

DID YOU KNOW?

Zane's elemental blade can generate frost and ice. It can fire freezing bolts and freeze things in place.

FALCON FRIEND

Zane's robot falcon was created by Zane's father, Dr. Julien, and first appears in LEGO® form in set 70724. It shares a special bond with Zane and can communicate with him in his dreams. The Stone Army captures it, but Zane soon stealthily swoops to the rescue!

ZANE'S NEWLY ENHANCED POWERS are as cool and icy as his new kimono-style ninja outfit. Armed with the double-edged Ice Blade, Zane is ready to freeze out the enemy—and he is able to produce an icy tornado powerful enough to knock even the Stone Warriors out cold!

GOLDEN NINJA
ULTIMATE SPINJITZU MASTER

NINJA FILE

LIKES: Defending Ninjago
DISLIKES: Catapults
FRIENDS: Golden Dragon
FOES: The Overlord
SKILLS: Summoning the Golden Dragon
GEAR: Golden Mech Sword, golden katana

KEY SET: Golden Mech (Legacy)
SET NUMBER: 71702
YEAR: 2020

Shoulder armor distinguishes this Golden Ninja from the variant found in a 2019 set

Green details hint at Lloyd's usual ninja identity

DID YOU KNOW?

The Golden Power is the most powerful elemental force in the Ninjago world. It can only be used by the Ultimate Spinjitzu Master.

THE GOLDEN TOUCH

This ancient fighting mech will only respond to the Golden Ninja's powers. Alongside the Golden Dragon, Lloyd finds it and awakens it in the Temple of Light.

Lloyd's seat in the cockpit is shaded by an oversized golden conical hat

LLOYD GARMADON becomes the Golden Ninja after his first battle with the Overlord. He is now the most powerful ninja of all. His shimmering golden robe and armor are symbolic of his status and his potential to harness the Golden Power. With this upgrade, he can overthrow the Overlord!

LORD GARMADON

DARK ISLAND MASTER

NINJA FILE

LIKES: Giving orders
DISLIKES: Light
FRIENDS: General Kozu
FOES: The Green Ninja
SKILLS: Managing the unruly Stone Army
GEAR: Mega-Weapon

KEY SET: Temple of Light
SET NUMBER: 70505
YEAR: 2013

Helmet of Shadows shows the Stone Army's scorpion claw symbol

Removable second torso gives extra height

Regular-size minifigure legs don't give any extra height

ISLAND OF DARKNESS

Lord Garmadon first reads about the Island of Darkness in the log of Captain Soto, the first captain of the *Destiny's Bounty*. Lord Garmadon soon grows determined to find this evil place.

THE FORMIDABLE Master of Darkness has not given up on his evil scheme to take over Ninjago Island. Under the guidance of the sinister Overlord, and looking more evil than ever, Lord Garmadon has revenge on his mind. He takes control of the Stone Army on the Island of Darkness, ready to attack.

OVERLORD
GOLDEN MASTER

Samurai helmet without chin guard attachment reveals alarming grin!

Rounded shoulder armor

NINJA FILE

LIKES: Inflicting pain, ruling Ninjago Island
DISLIKES: Losing a fight
FRIENDS: Overlords don't need friends
FOES: Everyone
SKILLS: Creating Stone Armies, flying
GEAR: Blade spear

KEY SET: The Golden Dragon (Legacy)
SET NUMBER: 70666
YEAR: 2019

A glowing purple energy core hints at the Overlord's true form

Ghostly lower body part in place of legs

ORIGINAL OVERLORD
Found in Battle for Ninjago City (set 70728), the 2014 Overlord has just two arms. His ethereal lower body is represented by unique printing on a standard minifigure skirt.

Serrated blade weapon with red ax head

FOR MANY YEARS, nobody knew what the Overlord looked like in physical minifigure form. He had been spotted only as a dark shadow—trying to defeat goodness and bring evil to the world. He finally manifested in 2014, then shapeshifted into an even spookier form in 2019!

NINJA FILE

LIKES: Bullying his troops
DISLIKES: Being chased by Zane's Ice Spider
FRIENDS: Lord Garmadon
FOES: Zane and the ninja
SKILLS: Multitasking at least four things at once
GEAR: Elemental ice blade

KEY SET: Golden Mech (Legacy)
SET NUMBER: 71702
YEAR: 2020

RED ALERT

Kozu's original minifigure wore more red—and an even more gruesome mask, complete with black fangs and batlike "ears." He is found in just one set, Garmatron (set 705045), from 2013.

Unusual butterfly swords

Fearsome helmet hides even more fearsome face

Shoulder armor is built into upper torso piece

DID YOU KNOW?
The Stone Army soldiers speak a mysterious language of their own. General Kozu acts as their translator.

Spiky chain mail hangs down from hips

GENERAL KOZU is Lord Garmadon's second-in-command in the Stone Army. An experienced warrior, he is especially fearsome when his four arms are wielding four weapons all at once. Kozu is in charge of mining for Dark Matter and likes to keep busy— he uses his extra limbs to bully his troops.

STONE ARMY SOLDIERS

STATUE SQUADRON

NINJA FILE

NAME: Stone Scout
KEY SET: The Golden Dragon (Legacy)
SET NUMBER: 70666
YEAR: 2019

Standard LEGO crossbow

Red shoulder armor is common in the Stone Army

As befits his rank, the warrior wears a winged helmet similar to Kozu's

2013 army had conical hats rather than rounded

Scouts have shorter legs than the other soldiers

NINJA FILE

NAME: Stone Warrior
KEY SET: Cole's Earth Driller (Legacy)
SET NUMBER: 70669
YEAR: 2019

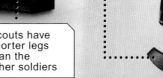

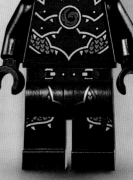

Green swirl pattern marks all of the troops in the Stone Army

NINJA FILE

NAME: Stone Swordsman
KEY SET: Cole's Earth Driller
SET NUMBER: 70502
YEAR: 2013

THE STONE ARMY was created by the Overlord. The army's tough warriors were built out of indestructible stone from the Underworld. As well as having rock-solid bodies, Stone Army soldiers are unbending in their obedience. These fearsome foes first marched in 2013 and were recalled for duty in Legacy sets from 2019 onward.

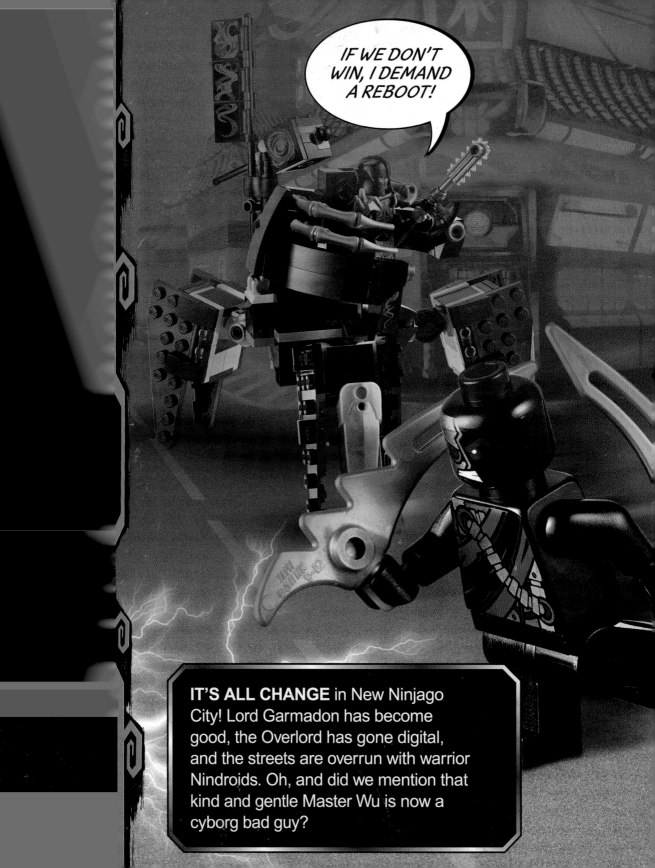

IF WE DON'T WIN, I DEMAND A REBOOT!

IT'S ALL CHANGE in New Ninjago City! Lord Garmadon has become good, the Overlord has gone digital, and the streets are overrun with warrior Nindroids. Oh, and did we mention that kind and gentle Master Wu is now a cyborg bad guy?

MASTER GARMADON

SPINJITZU MASTER REBORN

Simple bo staff used as a pointer in class, not for fighting

Natual hair color returns—now gray with age

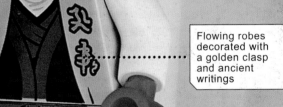

DID YOU KNOW?
Garmadon vows never to fight again in order to make up for all of his past evil actions. This vow is tested when the Nindroids arrive!

NINJA FILE

LIKES: Being good again
DISLIKES: His evil past
FRIENDS: Brother Wu
FOES: Digital Overlord
SKILLS: Teaching ninja
GEAR: Bo staff

KEY SET: Nindroid Mech Dragon
SET NUMBER: 70725
YEAR: 2014

Flowing robes decorated with a golden clasp and ancient writings

NINJA MENTOR
Dressed in variant robes from Ninja DBX (set 70750), Master Garmadon enjoys teaching the Art of the Silent Fist—a martial arts style involving misdirection and avoiding enemy attacks.

A tear in the back of the robes reveals a purple snake tattoo

COMPLETELY PURIFIED of evil, Garmadon transforms from a monster back into a man when the Overlord is seemingly defeated by Lloyd, the Golden Ninja. Garmadon's extra arms and dark-lord armor disappear, to be replaced by the ninja robes of a peace-loving Spinjitzu Master.

CYRUS BORG

POSSESSED COMPUTER GENIUS

CYRUS BORG
POSSESSED COMPUTER GENIUS

NINJA FILE

LIKES: Inventing gadgets
DISLIKES: Being controlled like a machine
FRIENDS: Techno Zane
FOES: The Overlord
SKILLS: Chasing
GEAR: Katana, saw

KEY SET: OverBorg Attack
SET NUMBER: 70722
YEAR: 2014

Remaining human eye glows with energy

Cybernetic eye is built into LEGO® hair piece

Saw-bladed weapon is common among the Nindroids

TOWN PLANNER

After the first defeat of the Overlord, Cyrus Borg strove to make Ninjago Island a center of technological advancement. He rebuilt Ninjago City and named it "New Ninjago City."

A spider-limbed mech transports the OverBorg around Ninjago

CYRUS BORG is an inventor, computer genius, and upstanding Ninjago citizen. But a bite from Pythor turns him into a cyber robot, controlled by the now-digital Overlord. Transformed into OverBorg, he uses his technological skills to summon the Nindroid Army in an attempt to rule Ninjago Island.

TECHNO COLE
REBOOTED EARTH NINJA

New robes for Legacy version of Techno Cole

NINJA FILE

LIKES: New technology
DISLIKES: Hover Hunters
FRIENDS: Techno ninja
FOES: General Cryptor
SKILLS: Converting Security Mechs into Earth Mechs
GEAR: Techno-Hammer

KEY SET: Thunder Raider (Legacy)
SET NUMBER: 71699
YEAR: 2020

Hammer made from six LEGO elements

COLE'S EARTH MECH
Cole pilots his Earth Mech from a small cockpit at the top of the huge robot and fires missiles at his foes from the sword blasters on its arms.

DID YOU KNOW?
The Techno Blades can hack into computer systems and transform ordinary machinery into awesome high-tech ninja vehicles.

High-powered sword blaster

DRESSED IN HIS STYLISH black Techno robes, with a matching bandana to help block facial-recognition software, Cole is ready to battle his latest enemy, the Nindroids. He loves a challenge and will push his ninja skills to their limits using the new Techno gear—including his hammer and mighty mech.

TECHNO KAI
REBOOTED FIRE NINJA

Silver katana sword found in more than 50 LEGO sets

DID YOU KNOW?
The 2020 Legacy Kai Fighter set has 317 more pieces than the 2014 version of the set!

Bare arms help keep the Fire Ninja cool

NINJA FILE
LIKES: Transforming cars into weapons
DISLIKES: Insects
FRIENDS: Techno ninja
FOES: General Cryptor
SKILLS: Aiming missiles
GEAR: Red Techno Blade

KEY SET: Kai Fighter (Legacy)
SET NUMBER: 71704
YEAR: 2020

OLD FLAMES
The 2014 version of Techno Kai wore a realistic flame design on his long-sleeved red robes. He wielded the red Techno Blade in Kai Fighter (set 70721) and Ninja Charger (set 70727).

THE FLAME-SHAPED CLASP on Kai's Techno suit hints at his fiery fighting style. He wears a red bandana to hide his face, but his tousled hair is uncovered, just like all the Techno ninja. At the controls of his flying Kai Fighter, he is ready to face the sinister Nindroid Army.

TECHNO NINJA

REBOOTED HEROES

Legacy variant carries nunchuks instead of a Techno Blade

Lightning-bolt buckle keeps robe in place

Lloyd's blond hair piece makes its debut here

Electrical energy crackles beneath Zane's robes

Three Zane variants wield the blue Techno Blade

Golden Power emblem is also printed on Lloyd's back

THERE ARE FOUR TECHNO BLADES

in total, corresponding to the elements of Earth, Fire, Lightning, and Ice. That means Lloyd doesn't get one of his own, but he still gets Techno robes! The Techno Blades are not included with Legacy sets, where Jay and his friends rely on other weapons.

TECHNO WU

GOOD MASTER GONE BAD

Traditional conical hat now looks like it is made out of metal, not bamboo

Red robot eyes

Black and white robe displays cyber robot parts

VICTIM OF THE OVERLORD

The Overlord probes Master Wu's memory to find out where the ninja are hiding. He then turns Wu into his latest cyber drone victim—Techno Wu—and forces him to attack the ninja and Garmadon. This is a battle the ninja don't want to have to fight.

GONE ARE THE white kimono and beard of a kind teacher—poor Master Wu has been captured by the Overlord and transformed into an evil robot. In this variant, he wears black, befitting his new dark status. Have the ninja lost their beloved master forever?

P.I.X.A.L.
ACE ANDROID

The other side of P.I.X.A.L.'s face reveals a scowl and red eyes to show that she is under the Overlord's control

NINJA FILE

LIKES: Puzzles
DISLIKES: Nindroids
FRIENDS: Zane
FOES: Digital Overlord
SKILLS: Using technology
GEAR: Spike blade

KEY SET: NinjaCopter
SET NUMBER: 70724
YEAR: 2014

FRIENDS FOR LIFE
P.I.X.A.L. changes from cold and mechanical to loyal friend when Zane uses his Techno Blade to hack her programming. They go on to destroy many Nindroids together. When Zane is hurt, the two discover they are compatible and merge into one being—a move that saves Zane's life!

Spike blade is similar to the saw blades commonly used by Nindroids

P.I.X.A.L. IS SHORT FOR Primary Interactive X-ternal Assistant Life-form. She is a human-shaped robot, or android. While under the control of the Digital Overlord, she copies Zane's own android design to make the Nindroid Army. She is later freed from her programming and changes her ways.

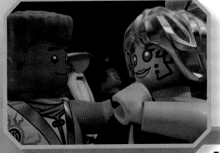

GENERAL CRYPTOR
LEADER OF THE NINDROID ARMY

Traditional ninja wrap upgraded with robot eyepiece

Ground-to-air laser rocket launcher

High-tech displays built into body armor

NINJA FILE

LIKES: Blabbering
DISLIKES: Getting kicked
FRIENDS: Nindroid Army
FOES: Kai and the ninja
SKILLS: Firing laser beams
GEAR: Laser rocket launcher, bazooka

KEY SET: Destructoid
SET NUMBER: 70726
YEAR: 2014

TECHNO TANK
General Cryptor controls his Destructoid battle tank from its 360-degree rotating command center. He unleashes lasers and missiles from the disk shooter and uses the razor-sharp chopping blades to attack the enemy.

SECOND-IN-COMMAND to the Overlord, the talkative and quick-tempered General Cryptor is the most powerful and advanced of the Nindroids, reflected by his unique armor. Cryptor believes himself to be the greatest warrior in the world and tends to severely underestimate his enemies!

NINDROID ARMY

OVERBORG'S MEAN MACHINES

NINJA FILE

NAME: Nindroid Drone
KEY SET: Hover Hunter
SET NUMBER: 70720
YEAR: 2014

Both eyes are artificial, but one looks more robotic than the other!

Striped sash worn under exterior cabling

NINJA FILE

NAME: Nindroid Warrior
SET NAME: Thunder Raider (Legacy)
SET NUMBER: 71699
YEAR: 2020

Nindroid mask covers same head piece used by Drone minifigure

Techno ax doubles as a chopper and a chainsaw!

Techno-Dagger sword

Mindroid is the only Nindroid with short minifigure legs

Striped sash worn over wiring and armor plating

NINJA FILE

NAME: Mindroid
KEY SET: Destructoid
SET NUMBER: 70726
YEAR: 2014

CONTROLLED BY THE OVERBORG
(who is in turn controlled by the Digital Overlord), the Nindroids are newer but not necessarily improved versions of Zane. They may be faster and stronger than the Master of Ice, but they lack his defining traits of honor and compassion.

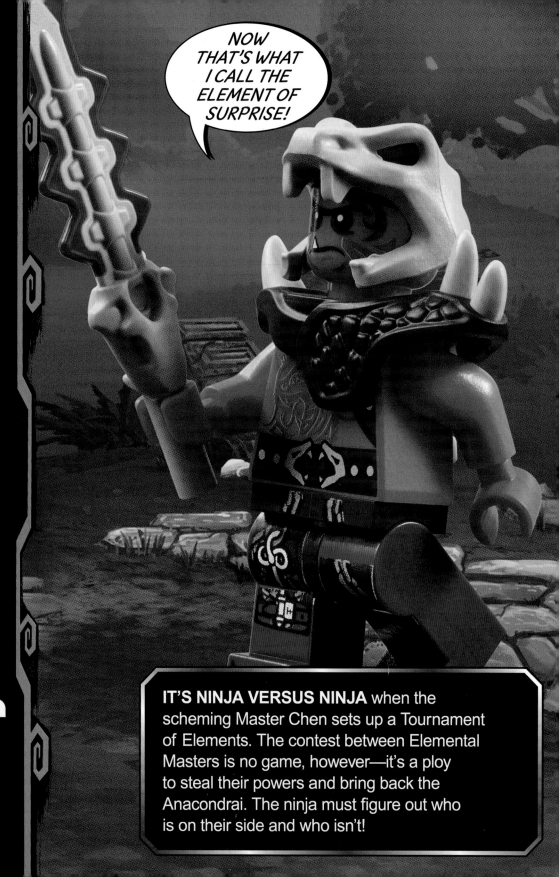

NOW THAT'S WHAT I CALL THE ELEMENT OF SURPRISE!

IT'S NINJA VERSUS NINJA when the scheming Master Chen sets up a Tournament of Elements. The contest between Elemental Masters is no game, however—it's a ploy to steal their powers and bring back the Anacondrai. The ninja must figure out who is on their side and who isn't!

Anacondrai skull and spine piece on head, with large purple snake around the skull

Distinctive face with mustache, goatee, and sideburns

Tooth necklace

NINJA FILE

LIKES: Wicked plans and complicated strategies
DISLIKES: Followers who are less intelligent than him
FRIENDS: Loyal Clouse
FOES: Non-Anacondrai
SKILLS: Tricking people
GEAR: Staff of Elements

KEY SET: Enter the Serpent
SET NUMBER: 70749
YEAR: 2015

Robe with gold trim and snake scale patterns

STAFF OF ELEMENTS

Chen's staff has the Power of Absorption—it takes the user's elemental power and stores it in a crystal orb. The elements can then be used by whoever holds it.

HOT-TEMPERED CHEN is a master of deception. He organizes the Tournament of Elements as a ruse to steal the powers of the Elemental Masters. With their powers, he plans to perform a spell that will turn his followers into Anacondrai—and then he will destroy Ninjago Island!

PYTHOR

ANACONDRAI SURVIVOR REBORN

Long, curved neck, unique among Serpentine

Jagged, heavy blade can cut through jungle

NINJA FILE

LIKES: Peace and quiet
DISLIKES: Challenges to Serpentine race
FRIENDS: Noble ninja
FOES: New Anacondrai
SKILLS: Invisibility
GEAR: Bronze blade

KEY SET: Ninja DB X
SET NUMBER: 70750
YEAR: 2015

Head, body, and tail printing is now purple on a white background

CHANGING SIDES

When Pythor and Garmadon first met, they were both enemies of the ninja. By the time of the Tournament of Elements, Garmadon fights on the side of good, and Pythor learns to change his ways, too!

A SPELL IN THE STOMACH of the Great Devourer has turned Pythor a ghostly white. Now Master Chen wants to capture Pythor and use his sweat to create his own Anacondrai warriors! Pythor isn't keen on the idea, and might just have to team up with the ninja ....

SKYLOR

ELEMENTAL MASTER OF AMBER

NINJA FILE

LIKES: The color red, mostly on Kai

DISLIKES: Devilish dads

FRIENDS: Kai

FOES: Anacondrai

SKILLS: Can absorb others' elemental powers

GEAR: Crossbow

KEY SET: Condrai Copter Attack

SET NUMBER: 70746

YEAR: 2015

Arrow and quiver

Symbol represents the number six—could Skylor become the sixth ninja?

DID YOU KNOW?

Skylor's mother was the previous Elemental Master of Amber, but no one knows what happened to her or where she has gone.

Knee pads on leg piece

FAMILY TIES

During the tournament, the ninja find out that Skylor is the daughter of Master Chen. When Skylor finds out how evil her father really is, she is torn between her loyalty toward her family and doing the right thing.

SKYLOR'S ROBES reflect the elemental power of Amber. This allows her to absorb other powers through touch and make use of them herself. A trained ninja and highly skilled with the bow and arrow, Skylor enters the Tournament of Elements. But can she be trusted?

TOURNAMENT KAI

FIERCE AND FIERY COMPETITOR

NINJA FILE

LIKES: Winning
DISLIKES: Secrets
FRIENDS: Skylor
FOES: Karlof, Chen
SKILLS: Building trust
GEAR: Kama blade, Jade Blades

KEY SET: Tournament of Elements (Legacy)
SET NUMBER: 71735
YEAR: 2020

DID YOU KNOW?
A kama is a traditional Japanese farming tool and martial arts weapon. It is sometimes known as a kai!

Robe closed with a flame-shaped clasp

Kama can be swapped for a range of Jade Blades

JADE SHADES
The Legacy version of the tournament dojo includes all-new Jade Blades in various shapes and sizes. Unlike the 2015 blades, they are bright green all over rather than gold with transparent green tips.

DRESSED IN THE SLEEVELESS ROBES
given to him by Chen, Kai is ready to enter the Tournament of Elements. The robe is light—ideal for ninja battle moves—but has a padded chest plate for protection. Kai is quick to enter the competition and does not stop to think about Chen's motives.

TOURNAMENT COLE

TRICKED, THEN TRAPPED

NINJA FILE

LIKES: Reuniting with friends

DISLIKES: Mysterious trapdoors leading to prison, meals involving noodles

FRIENDS: Zane

FOES: Chen's henchmen

SKILLS: Escaping jail

GEAR: Scythe Jade Blade

KEY SET: Lava Falls

SET NUMBER: 70753

YEAR: 2015

Matching black bandana to disguise face

Scythe Jade Blade

Ninja gi decorated with chest strap shows the elemental symbols of Kai, Cole, Jay, and Lloyd

FACTORY FLYER

When Cole is knocked out of the Tournament of Elements, Chen steals his powers and puts him to work in his noodle factory. The Earth Ninja escapes by using the factory facilities to build a Boulder Blaster plane (Legacy set 71736).

ARMED WITH A SCYTHE JADE BLADE, and all in black, Cole looks as serious as ever. With planned moves and strategic thinking, Cole combines his weapon skills and strength to show the competition what he is made of. However, he will need more than new robes to get out of Chen's trap!

TOURNAMENT JAY

UNLUCKY IN LOVE

Spear Jade Blade

NINJA FILE

LIKES: Defeating evil
DISLIKES: Fighting with his friends
FRIENDS: Nya
FOES: Cole, Chen
SKILLS: Extreme speed and agility
GEAR: Spear Jade Blade

KEY SET: ElectroMech
SET NUMBER: 70754
YEAR: 2015

DID YOU KNOW?

The Legacy variant of Tournament Jay wields nunchuks in 2021's Tournament of Elements (set 71735).

LOVE FEUD

When Jay discovers that Cole has feelings for Nya, too, he is angry with his friend. Chen takes advantage of this situation and pits the two ninja against each other in the tournament. From Chen's point of view, that takes two more ninja out of action.

Printing on leg piece shows robe sash and knee stripes

JAY'S NEW LIGHT AND FLEXIBLE tournament robe is the perfect outfit to show off his ninja speed and agility in the competition arena. His opponents had better watch out—wielding his spear Jade Blade, Jay is a formidable combatant, both in and out of the tournament arena.

TOURNAMENT LLOYD

JUNGLE-BOUND

DID YOU KNOW?

Tournament Lloyd gets a Legacy upgrade with green eyes in Boulder Blaster (set 71736) from 2021.

Flail Jade Blade is a nunchuk-style weapon

JUNGLE RAIDER

Lloyd's cool, green off-roader, with its large, spiked wheels, is the perfect vehicle to travel through the rough terrain of the jungle. Armed with front shooters, the Green Ninja can battle the sneaky Anacondrai tribe.

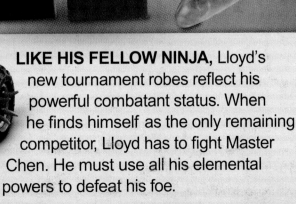

LIKE HIS FELLOW NINJA, Lloyd's new tournament robes reflect his powerful combatant status. When he finds himself as the only remaining competitor, Lloyd has to fight Master Chen. He must use all his elemental powers to defeat his foe.

JUNGLE SAMURAI X
MASTER OF DISGUISE

NINJA FILE

LIKES: Surprise attacks
DISLIKES: Going undercover
FRIENDS: Fellow adventurer Dareth
FOES: Chen
SKILLS: Fooling everyone with disguises and stealth
GEAR: Black katanas

KEY SET: Ninja DB X
SET NUMBER: 70750
YEAR: 2015

Samurai helmet with gold ornamental spiked crest

Face guard for protection and to hide identity

Nya's alternative samurai robe, and body armor is green with gold flames and a phoenix emblem

KABUKI SPY

Resourceful Nya is a master of stealth and disguise. Dressed as a theatrical Kabuki performer, she sneaks into Chen's palace to find out what he is up to and to make contact with the ninja.

ON THE RUN FROM CHEN, his minions, and their Anacondrai transformation spell, Nya dons her fearsome-looking samurai armor and escapes into the jungle. She must find the ninja and warn them about Chen's evil plans. Leaving a fake trail of footprints, Nya eludes the enemy!

KARLOF

ELEMENTAL MASTER OF METAL

NINJA FILE

LIKES: Shiny metals
DISLIKES: The thought of losing a fight
FRIENDS: Opponent Cole
FOES: Thieving Skylor
SKILLS: Power-packed punching, engineering
GEAR: Metallic fists

KEY SET: Dojo Showdown
SET NUMBER: 70756
YEAR: 2015

Samurai helmet

Shoulder pad armor with scabbard for two katana swords

Metal fists also worn by Gorillas in LEGO® Legends of Chima™ sets

Silver metal body armor worn over black robe

FIRST ONE OUT

Karlof loses to Kai in the first round of the tournament when Kai craftily steals the Jade Blade from him. He is taken to a secret underground room where Chen drains his metal power. Defenseless, Karlof is then set to work in Chen's Noodle Factory.

WHAT BRUTISH KARLOF lacks in ninja fighting skills, he makes up for with his strength and stamina. He can turn his body into hard metal and his hands into giant metal fists—all of which enhances his punching power! Karlof comes from Metalonia, where he worked as a mechanic and an engineer.

NINJA FILE

LIKES: Winning races
DISLIKES: Delays
FRIENDS: Ninja
FOES: That cheater Chen
SKILLS: Awesome speed, kickboxing
GEAR: Bo staff

KEY SET: Dojo Showdown
SET NUMBER: 70756
YEAR: 2015

Dual-sided head (angry face without shades on reverse)

Griffin wields a sturdy staff as his weapon

Kimono has "go-faster" stripes

FASTER THAN FAST
Griffin likes to show off his elemental power and is extremely competitive with the ninja. However, when he finds out what Chen is really up to, he joins forces with the heroes.

DID YOU KNOW?
After the core ninja team, Griffin, Karlof, and Skylor were the first Elemental Masters to appear in minifigure form.

BLINK AND YOU'LL MISS HIM! Griffin Turner can run at incredible speeds. In his red sunglasses and his kimono adapted for running, Griffin thinks he is one cool dude. He makes it through several rounds of the Tournament of Elements, until he is tricked by Chen and has his powers drained.

ELEMENTAL MASTERS

TOURNAMENT CONTENDERS

NINJA FILE

NAME: Gravis
KEY SET: Tournament of Elements (Legacy)
SET NUMBER: 71735
YEAR: 2021

Plants spring from staff on Bolobo's command

Floating necklace casts a shadow on robes

Fab gear projects a retro rock star image

Sparkling gravitational energy flows from hands

NINJA FILE

NAME: Bolobo
KEY SET: Tournament of Elements (Legacy)
SET NUMBER: 71735
YEAR: 2021

Guitar doubles as a makeshift weapon

Bare chest decorated with ancient symbols

NINJA FILE

NAME: Jacob
KEY SET: Tournament of Elements (Legacy)
SET NUMBER: 71735
YEAR: 2021

THESE ELEMENTAL MASTERS all compete in the Tournament of Elements. Gravis is the Master of Gravity and can make heavy objects lighter than air. Bolobo is the Master of Nature and has the power to control plants. Jacob is the Master of Sound and can make a lot of noise!

TITANIUM ZANE
ICE NINJA REBUILT

NINJA FILE

LIKES: Embracing his new powers
DISLIKES: Nightmares
FRIENDS: Titanium Dragon
FOES: Clouse
SKILLS: Unleashing the Titanium Dragon
GEAR: Golden sai, katanas

KEY SET: Titanium Dragon
SET NUMBER: 70748
YEAR: 2015

Titanium shoulder pad armor with scabbard for two katana swords

Ninja zukin is a headwrap showing Zane's elemental symbol

Two shurikens slot under titanium belt

TWICE TITANIUM

The new improved Titanium Zane has a dual-sided head with two Nindroid faces. One shows a happy, silver robot face with blue eyes, while the other shows a serious Zane with a protective blue visor and robotic eyepiece.

THOUGH HIS FELLOW NINJA thought he had been destroyed by the Golden Master, Zane survived in digital form. Over time, he was able to rebuild himself as the Titanium Ninja, complete with cool new armor. Now Zane is shinier than ever and ready to reunite with his friends!

CLOUSE

MASTER CHEN'S SECOND-IN-COMMAND

DID YOU KNOW?
Clouse went on to plague the ninja as a ghost, but his spectral form has never been made into a minifigure.

NINJA FILE

LIKES: Spine-chilling spells
DISLIKES: The Cursed Realm
FRIENDS: Master Chen— he gives free noodles!
FOES: Garmadon
SKILLS: Sorcery
GEAR: Pike, Book of Spells

KEY SET: Titanium Dragon
SET NUMBER: 70748
YEAR: 2015

Snake fangs pattern on armor

Pike with four side blades

CHEN'S STUDENT

Clouse studied alongside young Garmadon under the training of Master Chen. When a duel broke out between the two students, Chen declared that the winner would become his right-hand man. Garmadon cheated and Clouse lost, for which Clouse never forgave him.

THE SINISTER, PURPLE-ROBED CLOUSE is a master of dark magic. He is a member of Chen's Anacondrai Army and proudly wears armor decorated with snake heads and fangs. Once Chen possesses all the elements, Clouse will use dark magic to transform Chen's followers into Anacondrai.

EYEZOR

CHIEF ANACONDRAI WARRIOR

NINJA FILE

LIKES: Spreading fear
DISLIKES: Words—less talk, more action
FRIENDS: None. You can't beat up friends, can you?
FOES: Furious Kai
SKILLS: Bullying
GEAR: Anacondrai Blade

KEY SET: Condrai Copter Attack
SET NUMBER: 70746
YEAR: 2015

Mohawk hair piece instead of the snake helmet worn by all other army members

Leather vest with snake-head belt buckle

Eyezor's Anacondrai Blade is a bone sword with jagged purple edges

Silver punk chains and buckles printed on legs

CONDRAI COPTER CHASE!

Eyezor pursues Skylor through the jungle in the fearsome-looking Condrai Copter, with its adjustable wings for flight or attack mode. Firing missiles, he swoops down to drop a net over his victim.

Huge net shoots out from vehicle's "mouth"

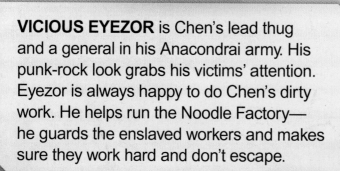

VICIOUS EYEZOR is Chen's lead thug and a general in his Anacondrai army. His punk-rock look grabs his victims' attention. Eyezor is always happy to do Chen's dirty work. He helps run the Noodle Factory—he guards the enslaved workers and makes sure they work hard and don't escape.

ANACONDRAI CULT

CHEN'S FAKE SNAKE FACTION

Spiky shoulder armor marks Zugu out as a general

NINJA FILE

NAME: Zugu
KEY SET: Boulder Blaster
SET NUMBER: 70747
YEAR: 2015

NINJA FILE

NAME: Krait
KEY SET: Anacondrai Crusher
SET NUMBER: 70745
YEAR: 2015

Scar running over lips

Anacondrai Blade is the main weapon used by the Anacondrai Army

NINJA FILE

NAME: Sleven
KEY SET: Lava Falls
SET NUMBER: 70753
YEAR: 2015

Fang-shaped dagger

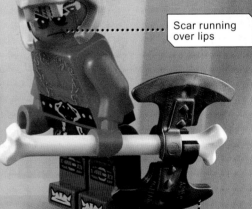

Double-bladed bone ax

Symmetrical snake tattoos and belt buckle design

ANACONDRAI CULTISTS such as Zugu and Krait don't just like snakes—they want to become snakes! Cautious Sleven is not so keen on the idea, but he is still devoted to Master Chen. And so each cultist slithers ever closer to transforming into a serpent in one of Clouse's rituals ....

CHÓPE'RAI
CHOPE TRANSFORMED

NINJA FILE

LIKES: Slithering around
DISLIKES: His new slippery purple skin
FRIENDS: Kapau'rai
FOES: Master Wu—for organizing their defeat
SKILLS: Leading attacks
GEAR: Anacondrai Blade

KEY SET: Titanium Dragon
SET NUMBER: 70748
YEAR: 2015

Shoulder pad armor decorated with fang spikes

Bone sword with sharp, jagged edges on the blade

DID YOU KNOW?
The fake Anacondrai are eventually banished to the Cursed Realm by some real Anacondrai ghosts, summoned by Wu.

FAKE SNAKE
Before becoming Chope'rai, Chope wears face tattoos and a snake-skull helmet to make himself more like a true Anacondrai. His human form is found in just one set, 2015's ElectroMech (set 70754).

Snake tattoo and chest muscles on torso

THE ANACONDRAI HAVE RETURNED!
Using Pythor's sweat, Clouse transforms Master Chen's human followers into snakes. Chope becomes the sly, blade-wielding serpent Chope'rai, on a mission to help Chen take over Ninjago. Will the Elemental Masters be able to defeat this new fearsome enemy?

KAPAU'RAI
KAPAU TRANSFORMED

New head
and tail
pieces
identical to
Chope'rai's

DID YOU KNOW?
For the warriors'
transformation to be
permanent, they needed
the sweat of a true
Anacondrai.

One red arm,
just like his
original form

Metallic snake
scales on center
of torso

SOLDIER TO SERPENT
Compare Kapau with Kapau'rai
and you'll spot a similar body
armor and belt design. Only his
spiked shoes and helmet
go astray when he
transforms into
a snake!

WITH CLOUSE'S MAGIC, Anacondrai cultist
Kapau achieves his dream and becomes
the terrifying armored snake, Kapau'rai.
With fangs bared and tail pieces on trend
again, Kapau'rai follows his master into the
final showdown with the Elemental Masters
in the Corridor of Elders.

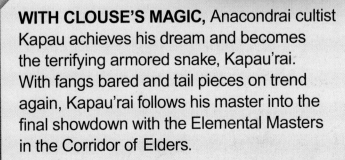

JUNGLE KAI
GOING ON A SNAKE HUNT

NINJA FILE

LIKES: Playing hide and seek in the jungle

DISLIKES: Anyone who turns against their friends

FRIENDS: Skylor

FOES: Trickster Chen

SKILLS: Fooling Chen

GEAR: Golden swords

KEY SET: Anacondrai Crusher

SET NUMBER: 70745

YEAR: 2015

Bright red robes might not be best for hiding in the jungle!

Full-body gi with leather belt and chest pouch with fire emblem

Two kunai knives slot under leather scabbard chest strap

ELEMENTAL BOND
To Kai's overjoyed surprise, when he helps Skylor escape from her father, she finally admits that she has feelings for him in return.

KAI AND HIS NINJA COMRADES must battle the loathsome Anacondrai cultists in the thick jungle on Chen's unwelcoming island. Luckily, Kai's new lightweight gi and zukin hood provide the perfect outfit for creeping stealthily through the undergrowth to ambush the snake-loving scoundrels.

PREPARED FOR ANYTHING

Leather scabbard for two golden katana swords

NINJA FILE

NAME: Jungle Lloyd
KEY SET: Enter the Serpent
SET NUMBER: 70749
YEAR: 2015

Map with directions to Anacondrai temple

One of two golden sai

NINJA FILE

NAME: Jungle Jay
KEY SET: Enter the Serpent
SET NUMBER: 70749
YEAR: 2015

NINJA FILE

NAME: Jungle Cole
KEY SET: Boulder Blaster
SET NUMBER: 70747
YEAR: 2015

Full-body gi with leather belt and chest pouch with lightning emblem

Ninja zukin showing Cole's elemental symbol

AS THE ANACONDRAI CULTISTS hide out in a hot and hazardous jungle, the ninja don mission-specific outfits to find them. Their new jungle gear combines lightweight robes with durable leather belts and pads. They are armed with weapons and other useful tools to navigate the environment.

Leather kneepads

THE GREEN NINJA becomes the mean ninja when a ghost named Morro takes control of his mind and body! Lloyd's friends will do anything to get him back to his normal self, even if that means being turned into spooks themselves ....

THIS CHAPTER IS SURE TO RAISE THE SPIRITS!

CHAPTER SIX

NINJA VS. GHOST NINJA

MORRO

GHOST ELEMENTAL MASTER OF WIND

Bandana to hide identity

Ninja gi bearing the Golden Power emblem

NINJA FILE

LIKES: Proving Wu wrong
DISLIKES: Taking selfies, losing the Realm Crystal
FRIENDS: Soul Archer
FOES: Lloyd
SKILLS: Airjitzu
GEAR: Howling Whip

KEY SET: Final Flight of Destiny's Bounty
SET NUMBER: 70738
YEAR: 2015

Ragged black cape

PERFECT STUDENT

Morro was Master Wu's first student. He soon mastered the martial arts and Wu thought that he might be the prophesied Green Ninja. When it became clear that he wasn't, Morro became obsessed with proving Wu wrong.

Transparent green ghost legs

BACK FROM THE CURSED REALM as a ghost, Morro is set on revenge against Wu and the ninja. Driven by jealousy, Morro uses his cunning and mastery of his element, the wind, to possess Lloyd and attack the other ninja. His mission is to bring evil to Ninjago Island once again.

DEEPSTONE LLOYD

WAGING GHOST WARS

Double-layered, two-colored zukin headwrap

Green Ninja's elemental symbol on front of torso

Straps and belt in Lloyd's personal color

DEEPSTONE STYLE

Lloyd's Deepstone minifigure appears in two sets. He comes with his new zukin headwrap and his distinctive blond hair piece for two interchangeable looks.

HAVING DEFEATED MASTER CHEN, Lloyd and his fellow ninja must now face the treacherous Morro and his Ghost Ninja. Lloyd is fired up to save Ninjago Island from these ghoulish creatures, but is his new Deepstone armor enough to protect him from the dark forces at work?

EVIL GREEN NINJA

LLOYD POSSESSED!

Jagged-edged zukin headwrap with green bandana facemask attached

Sword of Sanctuary

FRIEND OR FOE?

The Evil Green Ninja attacks the *Destiny's Bounty* and tries to steal the Staff of the First Spinjitzu Master. In a battle with the other ninja, Kai briefly reminds Lloyd of his true self, but the moment passes and Morro regains control.

DID YOU KNOW?

The Sword of Sanctuary has the power of precognition, allowing anyone who holds it to see into the future.

LLOYD BECOMES the Evil Green Ninja when Morro possesses him. Manipulative Morro tricks Lloyd into a meeting at the Ninjago Museum of History and then takes control of his body. Lloyd takes on the ghoulish features of his possessor and wears sinister, tattered robes.

DEEPSTONE JAY
GHOST HUNTER

DID YOU KNOW?
The Aeroblades, circular shurikenlike weapons, have the ability to defeat the ghosts when they come into contact with them.

Two shurikens slot into belt

Deepstone Nunchuks

WALKER'S WHEELS
In Jay Walker One—the car he has named after himself—the Lightning Ninja is on a mission to find the Aeroblade. He must grab it before Morro's ghost troops turn him into a specter, too!

WIELDING HIS DEEPSTONE Nunchuks at lightning speed, Jay is a formidable force. Decked out in a sleek, protective robe and armor, Jay is calm and focused on his mission to get the Scroll of Airjitzu and take on the testing challenges of the Haunted Temple.

DEEPSTONE KAI

FIRE ON THE WATER

Zukin headwrap in Kai's signature color

Deepstone Scythe

NINJA FILE

LIKES: Saving Lloyd
DISLIKES: Water
FRIENDS: Possessed Lloyd
FOES: Morro
SKILLS: Trusting his friends
GEAR: Deepstone Scythe

KEY SET: Attack of the Morro Dragon
SET NUMBER: 70736
YEAR: 2015

DID YOU KNOW?

Mined from the ocean floor, Deepstone is the most effective material for making weapons that can combat water-fearing ghosts.

TOMB RAIDERS

In Attack of the Morro Dragon, Kai flies a streamlined jet board in pursuit of the Evil Green Ninja. He is determined to stop his foe from stealing the Realm Crystal from the tomb of the First Spinjitzu Master.

Kai's elemental symbol is on the front of torso

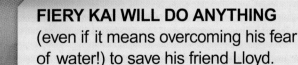

FIERY KAI WILL DO ANYTHING (even if it means overcoming his fear of water!) to save his friend Lloyd. Armed with his Deepstone Scythe, Kai sets course for the City of Stiix, intending to take the fight to Morro and his ghoulish army.

DEEPSTONE ZANE

NINDROID VS. GHOSTS

Aeroblade glows in the grasp of a trained ninja

Deepstone armor protects the wearer from being possessed by ghosts

TITANIC BATTLE

Sitting in the cockpit of his Titan Mech, Zane is set for the ultimate Mech battle. He uses the awesome weapons of his mighty machine to fight the terrifying four-armed Ghost Mech, Mech-enstein!

THE TITANIUM NINJA is back in style! As cool as his icy element in his new Deepstone gear, Zane pushes his superior robotic intelligence, stamina, and sixth sense to the max to outwit the ghostly enemy. With an Aeroblade at his command, Zane is armed and dangerous!

DEEPSTONE COLE

GHOST FIGHTER

Dual-colored zukin headwrap

Barrel cannon on each side of bike to blast ghosts

NINJA FILE

LIKES: Black armor
DISLIKES: Haunted temples
FRIENDS: Jay
FOES: Soul Archer
SKILLS: Conquering his fears to defeat ghosts
GEAR: Deepstone Scythe

KEY SET: Blaster Bike
SET NUMBER: 70733
YEAR: 2015

BORG-BUILT BIKE

Cole's one-of-a-kind motorcycle was built by Cyrus Borg for Cole to fight the Ghost Warriors.

A TRUE NINJA, Deepstone Cole is calm and focused, using his combat skills and great strength to defend his teammates against the terrifying Ghost Warriors. Overcoming his own fears, Cole always puts his friends' safety before his own.

One of two Deepstone swords in shoulder scabbard

Eyepatch with ghost-spotting scanner

NINJA FILE

LIKES: Stealing
DISLIKES: Losing bets
FRIENDS: Who needs friends when you can make money?
FOES: Everyone
SKILLS: Stealing, altering memories, piloting airships
GEAR: Stud shooters

KEY SET: Ronin R.E.X.
SET NUMBER: 70735
YEAR: 2015

R.E.X. FACTOR
Ronin is master of the skies in his awesome two-in-one airship. Equipped with an arsenal of weapons and a detachable Airjitzu flyer, Ronin is more than a match for the Ghost Warriors.

SEEMINGLY MOTIVATED BY money alone, Ronin does the dirty work of anyone willing to pay him. But when he winds up in the company of the ninja, their team spirit rubs off on him, and he uses his R.E.X. airship to help them in the fight against Morro's Ghost Ninja.

DEEPSTONE NYA
ELEMENTAL MASTER OF WATER

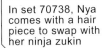

In set 70738, Nya comes with a hair piece to swap with her ninja zukin

Sashes with new elemental water emblem

VISION OF THE FUTURE
Before Nya has unlocked her elemental powers, Jay sees a vision of the pair's future. They both appear as experienced Elemental Masters. Future Jay appeared in minifigure form in 2018, but Future Nya appears for the very first time in this book!

DID YOU KNOW?
Elemental powers run in Nya's family! Nya inherited the elemental power of water from her mother, Maya.

NYA IS FULFILLING HER DESTINY! With Master Wu's guidance, Nya finds her inner ninja and learns to control her elemental power. Nya can now manipulate and generate water with her mind. She dives right into the battle against Morro and the ghosts—who happen to be afraid of water!

SOUL ARCHER

BOW MASTER

Zukin-style ninja headwrap with purple knotted bandana

NINJA FILE

LIKES: Capturing souls
DISLIKES: Being cheated
FRIENDS: Morro
FOES: Shady Ronin
SKILLS: Turning enemies to ghosts with deadly arrows
GEAR: Bow and arrow

KEY SET: Master Wu Dragon
SET NUMBER: 70734
YEAR: 2015

Shoulder pad armor with tattered robe draped over it

Transparent ghostly trail instead of leg piece

MORRO'S MAN

Soul Archer is Morro's right-hand man. Morro summoned him from the Cursed Realm for his arrow skills and nasty, no-nonsense nature to help him to get the Scrolls of Airjitzu.

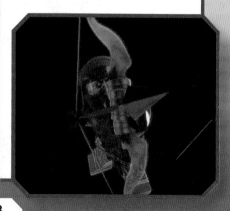

THIS GRUESOME GHOUL is an awesome archer—no other ghost can hit a target like the Bow Master. He can also create Skreemers by firing his arrows. If these creatures attach themselves to a human's head, the human will turn into a ghost.

GHOST MASTERS
MORRO'S MOST TRUSTED

Face printed on spooky transparent head

Wrayth has a ghost "tail" instead of legs in two sets

Tattered robe held together with chains

Shoulder armor and ragged vest are one multicolored piece

Headwrap is transparent at rear so eerie glow can shine through

NINJA FILE

NAME: Bansha
KEY SET: Jay Walker One
SET NUMBER: 70731
YEAR: 2015

NINJA FILE

NAME: Ghoultar
KEY SET: Ronin R.E.X.
SET NUMBER: 70735
YEAR: 2015

A variant Bansha has legs in Titan Mech Battle (set 70737)

ALONGSIDE SOUL ARCHER, these ghosts are Morro's most senior spooks. Wrayth is known as the Chain Master and wields a metal whip. Bansha owes her Blade Master name to her skill with spectral swords. Ghoultar is the Scythe Master, cutting a swath with his haunted reaper.

MING

GETTING IDEAS ABOVE HIS STATION

DID YOU KNOW?

Ming takes his work very seriously and has no patience for ghosts who think everything is fun and frights!

Transparent section in back of headwrap allows light to illuminate ghostly face from behind

Transparent leg piece with robe sash detail

Ghost Energy Blade

NINJA FILE

LIKES: Glowing green
DISLIKES: Stud shooters
FRIENDS: Cyrus
FOES: Nya, the Water Ninja
SKILLS: Flipping his blade
GEAR: Ghost Energy Blade

KEY SET: City of Stiix
SET NUMBER: 70732
YEAR: 2015

STIIX AND SCROLLS

When the ninja go to Stiix to find Ronin and the Scrolls of Airjitzu, Morro brings his warriors to the spooky city to ambush them. Employing his superior fighting skills, Ming leads the charge!

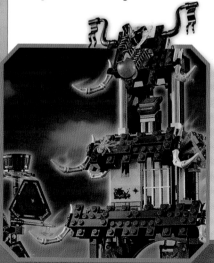

CLEVER AND SCARY, Ming is something of an expert on fighting techniques. The other ghosts come to him to get tips on how to fight and win outside of the Cursed Realm. Ming trains hard, and he is always trying to better himself. He may look the same as his fellow Ghost Ninja, but he feels very different.

GHOST NINJA

PHANTOM FORCE

No other soldier wields a spider-hilt saber!

NINJA FILE

NAME: Spyder
KEY SET: Final Flight of Destiny's Bounty
SET NUMBER: 70738
YEAR: 2015

Same ripped robe print as Ming and Wail

Ghoulish green katanas are new for 2015

NINJA FILE

NAME: Wail
KEY SET: Jay Walker One
SET NUMBER: 70731
YEAR: 2015

NINJA FILE

NAME: Cowler
KEY SET: Attack of the Morro Dragon
SET NUMBER: 70736
YEAR: 2015

All Ghost Ninja have transparent green legs

Unlike most Ghost Ninja, Wail has an opaque head

MORRO HAS A HOST OF GHOSTS under his command, many of whom can be hard to tell apart. Cowler could be mistaken for Cyrus, while Spyder looks a lot like Ming, Atilla, Hackler, and Yokai! Happily, to avoid confusion, not all of these spooky lookalikes have chosen to materialize here.

Kama blade is a kind of sickle

AIRJITZU KAI

SPINNING FIRE FLYER

New ninja robe with
flame pattern and
Kai's elemental symbol
on the front

SPINJITZU TO AIRJITZU
Airjitzu is an extension of the
martial arts technique of Spinjitzu.
By tapping deeper into his
elemental energy, Kai is able to
create an airborne vortex of fire.

Blade of Wildfire has
two scythe blades (one
spiked, the other jagged)
and a burning fire sword

BY LEARNING THE ANCIENT ART of Airjitzu,
Kai has reached a higher level of his true ninja
potential. His new flame-patterned robe reflects
this elevated status. Focusing on the power of
his fire energy, Kai creates a tornadolike vortex
around himself and levitates over the land. Maybe
now the ninja will be a match for the ghosts.

AIRJITZU NINJA

FLYING FIGHTERS

Unique blue head piece with lightning patterns around the eyes

Electro torch

Double-headed Cleaver with two scythelike blades

NINJA FILE

NAME: Airjitzu Jay
KEY SET: Airjitzu Jay Flyer
SET NUMBER: 70740
YEAR: 2015

NINJA FILE

NAME: Airjitzu Zane
KEY SET: Airjitzu Zane Flyer
SET NUMBER: 70742
YEAR: 2015

Broken rock pattern continues onto legs

NINJA FILE

NAME: Airjitzu Cole
KEY SET: Airjitzu Cole Flyer
SET NUMBER: 70741
YEAR: 2015

Polearm Ice Sword with added jagged scythe blade

Ninja robe with ice shard pattern

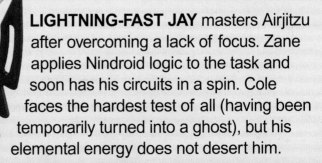

LIGHTNING-FAST JAY masters Airjitzu after overcoming a lack of focus. Zane applies Nindroid logic to the task and soon has his circuits in a spin. Cole faces the hardest test of all (having been temporarily turned into a ghost), but his elemental energy does not desert him.

TEMPLE WU

TEA EXPERT

NINJA FILE

LIKES: Serving tea
DISLIKES: Coffee
FRIENDS: Misako
FOES: The Preeminent
SKILLS: Giving advice
GEAR: Teapot. It only appears harmless.

KEY SET: Temple of Airjitzu
SET NUMBER: 70751
YEAR: 2015

DID YOU KNOW?

Master Wu's tea shop is called Steep Wisdom. It is located in a valley on Ninjago Island and has a tea farm and pond.

Long, gold sleeveless vest over robe with golden flower symbol on back of torso

Elaborate design continues onto legs

BACK IN ACTION

In Master Wu Dragon (set 70734), another version of Wu wields a Deepstone staff in one hand and a flaming teapot in the other. He also has a new pet dog to carry his crossbow!

AFTER MANY YEARS of mentoring and teaching, the ever-patient Wu is happy to hang up his fighting robes. His stylish long vest and gi are perfect for relaxing in the new tea shop he runs with Misako. Retirement seems to be suiting Wu well, but will he be allowed to enjoy a simpler life for long?

MISAKO

ARTY ARCHAEOLOGIST

Gray hair piece has a long French braided ponytail

Lines around eyes indicate a life spent smiling and squinting at ancient artifacts!

Practical safari suit with green neckerchief and roomy pockets

NINJA FILE

LIKES: Painting
DISLIKES: Interruptions—an artist needs their space
FRIENDS: Wu
FOES: Ghosts and ghouls
SKILLS: Guiding ninja against ghosts
GEAR: Paintbrush

KEY SET: Temple of Airjitzu
SET NUMBER: 70751
YEAR: 2015

HIDDEN TALENT

Misako is a keen painter. When she's not researching history, helping Wu teach the ninja, or working in the tea shop, Misako relaxes by taking up her brush and putting paint to canvas. The huge Temple of Airjitzu set includes her artist's studio.

ARTISTIC MISAKO works at the Ninjago Museum of History as an archaeologist and researcher. When the ninja go to Ninjago City to face the new Stone Army, they meet Misako and discover that she is actually Lloyd's mother and Lord Garmadon's long-lost wife!

NINJAGO MAILMAN
EXPRESS DELIVERY

NINJA FILE

LIKES: Delivering mail
DISLIKES: Climbing steps
FRIENDS: Pen pals
FOES: E-mail users
SKILLS: Alarming ninja by ringing the bell in the middle of an attack
GEAR: Stylish satchel

KEY SET: Temple of Airjitzu
SET NUMBER: 70751
YEAR: 2015

DID YOU KNOW?
The mailman is a recurring background character in the NINJAGO® TV series, but appears for the first time as a minifigure in the Temple of Airjitzu set.

Purple jacket features mail horn logo

WELCOME BREAK
In the Temple of Airjitzu, the mailman is one of the many minifigures to enjoy watching a shadow-puppet show. He sits alongside the ninja, Claire, and Jesper.

Letter tile with an elaborate signature

TRULY DEDICATED TO HIS JOB, the mailman goes beyond the call of duty to deliver mail to the ninja. No mountain is too high, no terrain too dangerous or bizarre, and no hideout too secret for this tireless postal hero. By air or by sea, no delivery is too distant. He is definitely a first-class guy!

DARETH

MASTER OF CHARM

> Coiffed, glossy hair is Dareth's crowning glory!

NINJA FILE

LIKES: Bragging
DISLIKES: Messing up his hair
FRIENDS: Jesper
FOES: Ghosts
SKILLS: Charming others
GEAR: Immaculate hair

KEY SET: Temple of Airjitzu
SET NUMBER: 70751
YEAR: 2015

> Charming smile

DID YOU KNOW?

Dareth once toured Ninjago Island as a singer with a show called "Brown Suede Shoes."

> New ninja robes with star pendant and star emblem on back of torso, and elaborate gold trim

MEDALLIAN MAN

The first Brown Ninja minifigure appears in 2014's small Dareth vs. Nindroid set (5002144). Dareth carries a large trophy he has awarded himself for imaginary martial arts achievements!

DARETH CLAIMS TO BE a martial arts master. He meets the ninja when they train in his dojo, and they soon realize he has no fighting skills at all! Despite his bragging, Dareth is a likeable guy and a loyal friend. What he lacks in real ninja skills, he makes up for with his creativity and smooth charm.

Catch of the day!

Outback-style cowboy hat worn with neckerchief

Casual safari-style shirt with smiley face badge on pocket

NINJA FILE

LIKES: A tidy garden
DISLIKES: Dirty ponds
FRIENDS: Funny Dareth
FOES: Ghosts
SKILLS: Fishing
GEAR: Fishing rod, and sometimes a fish

KEY SET: Temple of Airjitzu
SET NUMBER: 70751
YEAR: 2015

Protective apron covered in stains

FISHERMAN'S FRIEND

Jesper is a good friend of Dareth's. The competitive fishing pals can never agree on who has caught the biggest fish!

JESPER SPENDS his days keeping the Temple of Airjitzu shiny and clean. In his spare time, he enjoys searching for the best fishing spots on Ninjago Island and trying to catch the biggest fish ever. His minifigure is decked out accordingly and well suited for the great outdoors.

CLAIRE

ADVENTUROUS ASSISTANT

Claire keeps a careful eye out for parts of the temple that might need repairs

This amulet-style necklace might bring good luck and ward off ghosts!

NINJA FILE

LIKES: Shadow-puppet shows at the temple
DISLIKES: Cobwebs
FRIENDS: Ninja, Jesper
FOES: Intruders
SKILLS: Being brave
GEAR: Glider vehicle

KEY SET: Temple of Airjitzu
SET NUMBER: 70751
YEAR: 2015

DID YOU KNOW?

Claire has never appeared in the NINJAGO TV series. Her minifigure was created especially for the Temple of Airjitzu set.

CLAIRE IN THE AIR

Claire's investigations inside the Temple of Airjitzu have turned up an antique glider. She bravely takes it for a spin around the temple grounds, much to the surprise of her father!

CLAIRE CAN'T WAIT to take over from her father, Jesper, as caretaker of the Temple of Airjitzu. She loves the fact that it might be haunted and spends as much time there as possible. If it wasn't for her handiwork, the place would be falling down by now!

NADAKHAN
CAPTAIN OF THE SKY PIRATES

NINJA FILE

LIKES: Breaking apart Ninjago Island
DISLIKES: Failing his father
FRIENDS: Sky Pirates
FOES: Ninja
SKILLS: Granting wishes
GEAR: Djinn Blade

KEY SET: Misfortune's Keep
SET NUMBER: 70605
YEAR: 2016

Genie-style hair piece

DID YOU KNOW?
The Djinn Blade belongs to the royal family of Djinjago. It can trap spirits inside of it, providing power to the wielder.

Sky Pirate skull-and-crossbones emblem

Extra torso incorporates two extra arms

Studded belt to match armor

Standard LEGO® pirate hook hand

Transparent orange genie tail

TRANSFORMATIVE POWERS
Monkey Wretch was once a skilled human ship mechanic before Nadakhan tricked him into wishing for more hands and more speed and turned him into a mechanical monkey. Wretch does all the general repairs on Nadakhan's ship, *Misfortune's Keep*.

NADAKHAN, PRINCE OF DJINJAGO, is a djinn, a magical being who can grant wishes. He blames the ninja for the destruction of his homeland, Djinjago, and with his motley pirate crew in tow, he is now seeking revenge.

CLANCEE
SERPENTINE SKY PIRATE

NINJA FILE

LIKES: Swabbing the deck
DISLIKES: Heights, the sea
FRIENDS: Still looking
FOES: All of Captain Nadakhan's enemies
SKILLS: Evading traps
GEAR: Mop

KEY SET: Raid Zeppelin
SET NUMBER: 70603
YEAR: 2016

Padded shoulder pauldrons

Serpentine snake head with fangs

DID YOU KNOW?
Poor Clancee gets seasick and airsick—not great when you're a pirate sailing the high seas or whizzing through the air on a flying boat!

Rusty body armor and strap with ragged shirt displaying Sky Pirate emblem

WISHFUL THINKING
Clancee may not be the brightest crew member, but he knows Nadakhan is not to be trusted. By not asking for a wish, Clancee has probably, without even knowing it, saved his own scaly skin!

Simple, brown wooden peg leg

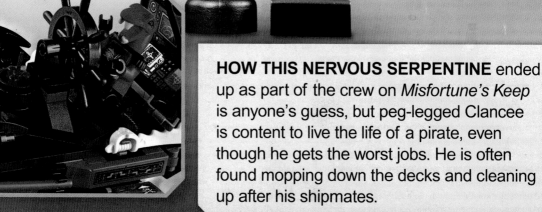

HOW THIS NERVOUS SERPENTINE ended up as part of the crew on *Misfortune's Keep* is anyone's guess, but peg-legged Clancee is content to live the life of a pirate, even though he gets the worst jobs. He is often found mopping down the decks and cleaning up after his shipmates.

FLINTLOCKE
SKY PIRATE FIRST MATE

Pilot goggles worn on top of green flying helmet

Separate bushy mustache piece

NINJA FILE

LIKES: His Sky Shark
DISLIKES: Secrets
FRIENDS: Nadakhan
FOES: Lloyd
SKILLS: Inspiring his crew to charge into battle
GEAR: Pistols

KEY SET: Sky Shark
SET NUMBER: 70601
YEAR: 2016

DID YOU KNOW?

Flintlocke's sleek Sky Shark jet serves as an advance scout vehicle for the Sky Pirates' flagship, the *Misfortune's Keep*.

Flintlocke wields two pirate pistols at once

FLYING FISH

With Flintlocke at the helm, the Sky Shark battle jet searches the skies for enemy aircraft. It then slices through the clouds with its anchor-shaped wings before the *Misfortune's Keep* arrives.

Mismatched legs covered in armor plating, straps, and buckles

FLINTLOCKE is Nadakhan's trusted right-hand man. He's loyal to his djinn captain and will follow him anywhere—as long as he knows where they're heading. But if he's expecting his leader to return his loyalty, then he's on the wrong ship!

Hidden dynamite drop function

DOGSHANK

HULKING SKY PIRATE

Horned helmet with built-in mouth visor, spiked pauldron, and skull emblem

NINJA FILE

LIKES: Fair fights
DISLIKES: Flintlocke's jokes
FRIENDS: Monkey Wretch
FOES: Nya
SKILLS: Twirling her anchor dangerously on a chain
GEAR: Ship's anchor

KEY SET: Tiger Widow Island
SET NUMBER: 70604
YEAR: 2016

Dogshank is the first "bigfig" (big figure) in LEGO® NINJAGO® sets

ON TIGER WIDOW ISLAND

Will Nya's stealthy ninja battle skills be enough to combat the brute strength and size of Dogshank? The pirate swings her weapon of choice, an anchor and chain, at the Master of Water as they fight.

BELIEVE IT OR NOT, the biggest of the Sky Pirates used to look like an everyday Ninjago citizen! But when she wished she could stand out in a crowd, Nadakhan turned Dogshank into an unmissable mass of muscles with a blue face—not what she had intended!

One bare arm where his uniform has been torn away

Alternative face print is this same mask turned upside-down

NINJA FILE

NAME: Sqiffy
KEY SET: Ninja Bike Chase
SET NUMBER: 70600
YEAR: 2016

One buckled boot and one worn-down steel-capped shoe

Epaulets replaced by armor in The Green NRG Dragon (set 70593)

Neck bracket for a scabbard worn on back

Cyren's expression can be changed from a grimace to a grin

NINJA FILE

NAME: Doubloon
KEY SET: Raid Zeppelin
SET NUMBER: 70603
YEAR: 2016

NINJA FILE

NAME: Cyren
KEY SET: Jay's Dragon
SET NUMBER: 70602
YEAR: 2016

THESE SKY PIRATES all found different ways into Nadakhan's crew. Doubloon was caught trying to steal the captain's gold and punished with a permanent mask. Cyren made a badly thought-out bargain with the Djinn and ended up as the ship's singer. And Sqiffy ... Sqiffy simply asked permission to come aboard!

DESTINY JAY
FEELING BLUE

NINJA FILE

LIKES: Helping his
ninja friends
DISLIKES: Making a wish!
FRIENDS: Zane
FOES: Nadakhan
SKILLS: Saving his friends
GEAR: Golden katanas

KEY SET: Jay's Elemental
Dragon
SET NUMBER: 70602
YEAR: 2016

Both eyes peek
out from beneath
Jay's headwrap

DID YOU KNOW?

When Jay wishes he'd
had a different start in life,
he learns that his real
father is the TV star
Cliff Gordon.

Cloth belt tie
ends with
golden clasps

SHIVER ME TIMBERS!

When the evil Nadakhan and his
fearsome band of Sky Pirates
kidnap Jay, he craftily disguises
himself as one of the brigands.
He then tries to escape before
they force him to walk the plank.

Eyepatch over
one eye is
Jay's pirate
disguise

CREATIVE JAY enjoys solving problems.
But when it comes to love, none of Jay's
inventions can fix his heartbreak. When Nya
tells Jay that she only wants to be friends
with him, the distraught ninja is tempted by
Nadakhan's dark wishes. However, he soon
discovers that love can't be won with a wish!

DESTINY NYA

DID YOU KNOW?

Nadakhan plans to trick Nya into marrying him. By doing so, he will secure ultimate power with unlimited wishes.

Red features on ninja gear are a throwback to Nya's Samuari X days

Blue emblem shows Nya's water powers

NINJA FILE

LIKES: Being part of a team
DISLIKES: Not being taken seriously
FRIENDS: Master Wu
FOES: Dogshank
SKILLS: Fighting Sky Pirates
GEAR: Golden katanas

KEY SET: Ninja Bike Chase
SET NUMBER: 70600
YEAR: 2016

MISSION POSSIBLE

Nya works with Wu to try and capture the Djinn Blade. If the heroes have the weapon, they might be able to save the spirits trapped inside it—and Nadakhan will lose some of his power!

AFTER MONTHS of intense training with Wu, Nya is now a fully fledged Master of Water and part of the team. She is fed up with all of the attention that the other ninja get and wants to be recognized for her skills in her own right. Time for Nya to strike out on her own!

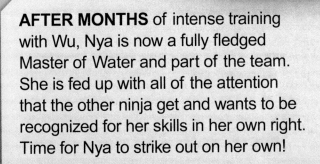

107

GHOST COLE
LIVING GHOST

Face now a ghostly green color

NINJA FILE

LIKES: Pulling Jay's leg
DISLIKES: Thermal vision
FRIENDS: Serious Lloyd
FOES: Dogshank
SKILLS: Quick thinking
GEAR: Katanas, scythe

KEY SET: Cole's Dragon
SET NUMBER: 70599
YEAR: 2016

DID YOU KNOW?

As a ghost, Cole has to learn how to make physical contact with objects and how to move through walls.

GHOST DRAGON RIDER

Even as a ghost, Cole is an awesome ninja. With Master Wu's guidance, he has relearned to control his elemental earth powers, and can call upon his new ghost dragon in battle.

Silver arms match headwrap and belt tie

AFTER A SERIES of unfortunate events in the Temple of Airjitzu, Cole has been turned into a ghost! With the help of his team, Cole is learning to accept his new living ghost form. The journey has not been easy, but Cole has tapped into his true ninja "spirit" and is now ready to face the latest threat to Ninjago.

DESTINY NINJA

DRESSED FOR SUCCESS

Each outfit shows an elemental creature in an Airjitzu whirlwind

Ornate knee-ties secure robes

NINJA FILE

NAME: Destiny Zane
KEY SET: Raid Zeppelin
SET NUMBER: 70603
YEAR: 2016

Single-shoulder armor makes its debut in 2016

New outfits are mostly black with elemental color used for details

NINJA FILE

NAME: Destiny Kai
KEY SET: Ninja Bike Chase
SET NUMBER: 70600
YEAR: 2016

NINJA FILE

NAME: Destiny Lloyd
KEY SET: Sky Pirate Jet
SET NUMBER: 70601
YEAR: 2016

Golden staff made from telescope, shuriken, and chainsaw pieces

Torso is also decorated with a winged symbol on the back

AFTER SAVING NINJAGO several times, the ninja are celebrities! As fans follow their every move, they treat themselves to some redesigned robes. However, the heroes still put function ahead of fashion. They may be on trend, but they are also on course to cross swords with the Sky Pirates!

ECHO ZANE

RUSTY REPLICA

NINJA FILE

LIKES: Finding out he has a "brother"

DISLIKES: Squeaky joints

FRIENDS: Tai-D

FOES: Clancee, Doubloon

SKILLS: Setting traps

GEAR: Staff

KEY SET: The Lighthouse Siege

SET NUMBER: 70594

YEAR: 2016

Face resembles Zane's, but in brass and copper colors

DID YOU KNOW?

Dr. Julien made Echo Zane to remind him of his greatest creation, his Nindroid "son," Zane.

Pressure valve shows that Echo Zane is partly steam-powered!

WIND-UP WARRIOR

When the Sky Pirates attack the Lighthouse Prison, Echo Zane helps Jay and Nya defend it. Though he lacks the ninja skills of the real Zane, he proves just as brave and loyal.

Rusty patches tarnish once shiny legs

JAY AND NYA MEET this clockwork copy of Zane in a disused Lighthouse Prison. They learn that the inventor Dr. Julien built Echo Zane for company when he was a prisoner there. Now the rusting robot lives there all alone! His clockwork cogs are visible through his battered outer casing.

TAI-D
MOBILE DRINK MACHINE

NINJA FILE

LIKES: Showing off his abilities
DISLIKES: Anyone getting in the way of his duties
FRIENDS: Echo Zane
FOES: Dust, dirt, and spills
SKILLS: Chess
GEAR: Tea tray

KEY SET: The Lighthouse Siege
SET NUMBER: 70594
YEAR: 2016

DID YOU KNOW?
Tai-D and the Lighthouse Prison were first seen in season two of the LEGO NINJAGO *Masters of Spinjitzu* TV series.

Magnifying goggles flip down for spotting the smallest speck of dust

Body made entirely from nonstandard minifigure parts

Front vents allow Tai-D to let off steam during the tea-making process!

TO MEND A FRIEND
Tai-D's duties also include keeping Echo Zane in working order. A basement workshop in the Lighthouse Prison includes an operation table where Tai-D can fine-tune his friend.

JUST LIKE HIS FRIEND Echo Zane, Tai-D is a robot made by Dr. Julien when he was held captive at the Lighthouse Prison. Tai-D's design might look simple, but his talents include making tea, cleaning, and even playing chess against Echo Zane. Clever Tai-D normally wins!

PRISONER ZANE
WRONGLY ARRESTED

Prisoner number starts "706," like most LEGO NINJAGO sets from 2016

Time in a cell does not diminish Zane's confident smile

NINJA FILE

LIKES: Planning his escape
DISLIKES: Being locked up with old enemies
FRIENDS: Captain Soto
FOES: Giant Stone Warrior
SKILLS: Food fighting
GEAR: Shurikens, bread roll

KEY SET: Kryptarium Prison Breakout
SET NUMBER: 70591
YEAR: 2016

FLUSHED OUT
The ninja (and their fellow inmate Captain Soto) escape prison through the sewers. That's why the toilet in the Kryptarium Prison Breakout set pops out of the wall!

DID YOU KNOW?
Ninjago criminals Lord Garmadon, Aspheera, Pythor, and Ronin have all been held in Kryptarium Prison.

ZANE BECOMES A PRISONER after the ninja are framed for crimes they didn't commit and sent to Kryptarium Prison. The white-and-gray-striped uniforms are an unwelcome change from traditional ninja robes, but at least they match Zane's classic color scheme! He is the only ninja to appear as a minifigure in his prison uniform.

KRYPTARIUM PRISON CREW

FACES FROM BOTH SIDES OF THE BARS

NINJA FILE

NAME: Prison Guard
KEY SET: Kryptarium
Prison Breakout
SET NUMBER: 70591
YEAR: 2016

Unique
skull-and-
wrenches
pirate symbol

Shades hide
a stern
expression

Stone Warrior
eyes can be
seen behind
mask

Officer's
uniform usually
found in LEGO®
City sets

One wooden
hand instead of
the traditional
pirate's hook

NINJA FILE

NAME: Giant Stone Warrior
KEY SET: Kryptarium
Prison Breakout
SET NUMBER: 70591
YEAR: 2016

NINJA FILE

NAME: Captain Soto
KEY SET: Kryptarium
Prison Breakout
SET NUMBER: 70591
YEAR: 2016

Spear is a
banned item
for prisoners!

THE NINJA HAVE PUT plenty of bad guys
in jail following their adventures. Some are
still in Kryptarium Prison when our heroes
are locked up there, too. From pirate
captains to members of the Overlord's
Stone Army, it's a reunion nobody
wanted—prison guards included!

MASTER YANG

SPOOKY SENSEI

Sunken eyes look jealously on the living

NINJA FILE

LIKES: Martial arts
DISLIKES: Being a ghost
FRIENDS: Chris and Martin
FOES: Nadakhan and the ninja
SKILLS: Turning people into ghosts
GEAR: Aeroblade

KEY SET: Airjitzu Battle Grounds
SET NUMBER: 70590
YEAR: 2016

MASTER WOOOOOO!

Like Master Wu, Yang is a seasoned dojo master eager to share a lifetime of skills. But Yang's teaching style is far too strict. He even traps his students inside his temple!

Long black beard covers training robes

A ghostly green wisp has replaced the legs Yang had as a mortal

THE INVENTOR OF AIRJITZU tried to live

forever but accidentally turned himself into a ghost instead. Now the once great teacher haunts his old temple, turning others into spirits like him. If only the ninja could make him see the error of his ways!

DID YOU KNOW?

The ninja traveled to Yang's temple in search of his written teachings—the fabled Scroll of Airjitzu.

114

YANG'S STUDENT

IS IT CHRIS OR MARTIN?

NINJA FILE

LIKES: Training
DISLIKES: Being chained up
FRIENDS: Other students
FOES: Dogshank
SKILLS: Airjitzu
GEAR: Staff, butterfly sword

KEY SET: Airjitzu Battle Grounds
SET NUMBER: 70590
YEAR: 2016

All of Yang's students have eerie green eyes

Plant tendrils grow through old robes

Airjitzu Battle Grounds is the only LEGO NINJAGO set to feature this headwrap in gray

ETERNAL PRACTICE

As ghosts, Chris and Martin have nothing better to do than play-fight in the Airjitzu Battle Grounds. It keeps them battle-ready just in case any real ninja show up.

DID YOU KNOW?

Yang's students all turn mortal again when they jump through the mystical Rift of Return with Cole.

MASTER YANG TRANSFORMED all of his Airjitzu students into ghosts, too. So much time has passed since that fateful day, that Yang can no longer tell the difference between Chris and Martin, two lookalike learners turned into identical gray-green spooks!

JUST REACHED THIS CHAPTER? IT'S ABOUT TIME!

THERE'S DOUBLE TROUBLE for the ninja when the Time Twins, Krux and Acronix, try to change the history of Ninjago. The villains' tools are four time-warping weapons and an entire army of slithering Serpentine known as the Vermillion!

GENERAL MACHIA

HEAD OF TAILS

Scary hair piece has five snake heads on the front and three on the back

NINJA FILE

LIKES: Turning her legs into a giant snake tail
DISLIKES: Bad hair days
FRIENDS: The Time Twins
FOES: Nya, Cyrus Borg
SKILLS: Mind control
GEAR: Vermillion ax

KEY SET: Samurai VXL
SET NUMBER: 70625
YEAR: 2017

SLITHER OR STRIDE?

In her only set appearance, Machia comes with a choice of standard minifigure legs or a brick-built lower body. The latter option makes her look more like a giant snake, towering head and shoulders over most other minifigures.

Torso print shows one of the many snakes that make up Machia's body

THE SUPREME COMMANDER of the Vermillion Army has been trained in fighting and strategy since the day she hatched. Like all the Vermillion Warriors serving under her, Machia is made up of hundreds of snakes in humanoid form. She really lets it show, with her squirming serpent hair!

DID YOU KNOW?

Machia's hair mold was first used for the LEGO® Minifigures theme in 2013. The Medusa Minifigure wore it in green!

ACRÓNIX
TECH-LOVING TIME TWIN

NINJA FILE
LIKES: Discovering modern technology
DISLIKES: Losing his elemental power
FRIENDS: Krux
FOES: Master Wu
SKILLS: Speeding up and slowing down time
GEAR: Time Blades

KEY SET: Dawn of Iron Doom
SET NUMBER: 70626
YEAR: 2017

Facemask obscures a lopsided grin and a wireless earpiece

DID YOU KNOW?
Acronix and Krux have been known as "the Elemental Masters of Time," "the Time Twins," and "the Hands of Time."

TIME BLADES
When Wu defeated the Time Twins, he transferred their powers into four elemental blades, then scattered the blades throughout time. But 40 years later, the Time Blades returned to the present, and Acronix and Krux seized their chance to rewrite the history of Ninjago!

Acronix always wears his cape on his left shoulder; Krux wears his on the right

MP3 player lets Acronix catch up on the last 40 years of music

Pause Time Blade

Forward Time Blade

Reversal Time Blade

Slo-Mo Time Blade

FORTY YEARS AGO, Acronix and his brother Krux tried to take over Ninjago using their powers as Elemental Masters of Time. When Wu stripped them of those powers and cast them into a time vortex, the brothers jumped in after them, and Acronix was transported 40 years into the future!

NINJA FILE

LIKES: Plotting
DISLIKES: The modern world
FRIENDS: Acronix
FOES: Master Wu
SKILLS: Pausing and reversing time
GEAR: Time Blades

KEY SET: Dawn of Iron Doom
SET NUMBER: 70626
YEAR: 2017

Red Time Blade lets Krux freeze an opponent in a single moment

DID YOU KNOW?

A twist of this minifigure's head reveals the bespectacled face of his amiable alter ego, Dr. Sander Saunders.

Clock hands and a sand timer on Krux's armor show his obsession with time

LONG-TERM PLANS

Krux did not waste his time as he waited for Acronix. Posing as the friendly Dr. Sander Saunders, he became curator of the Ninjago History Museum, while also secretly creating the Vermillion Army, designing and building a time-traveling mech, and kidnapping Kai and Nya's parents!

Orange Time Blade lets Krux make a target act in reverse!

WHEN THE TIME TWINS jumped into a temporal vortex, Krux was thrown just a few seconds into the future and had to wait 40 years for Acronix to arrive. Now he is decades older than his twin, who experienced his time in the vortex as the blink of an eye.

COMMANDER BLUNCK

MACHIA'S LEFT-HAND MAN

Shoulder armor and helmet both have snakehead designs

Vermillion ax head features a fanged serpent design

UNDER ARMOR
The back of Blunck's helmet hides a second facial expression, so he can be posed with his long tongue in or out. Underneath his ornate body armor, his double-sided torso print is a writhing mass of snakes!

BIG, BAD BLUNCK is one of the Vermillion's three commanding officers. His helmet allows him to control his troops with his thoughts, but sometimes those thoughts are on his dinner menu! He is one of the Vermillion's fiercest fighters—whether battling his enemies or arguing with his allies!

COMMANDER RAGGMUNK

MACHIA'S RIGHT-HAND MAN

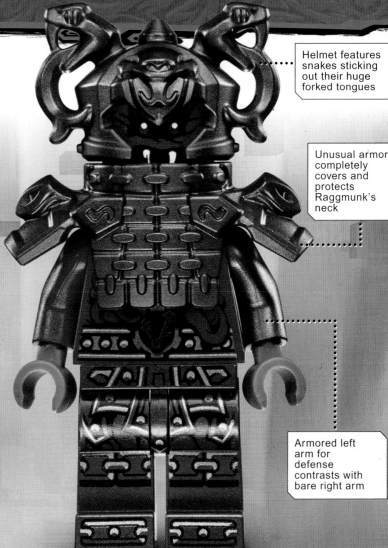

Helmet features snakes sticking out their huge forked tongues

Unusual armor completely covers and protects Raggmunk's neck

Armored left arm for defense contrasts with bare right arm

NINJA FILE

LIKES: Pleasing Krux and Acronix
DISLIKES: Getting a stiff neck from drafts
FRIENDS: Blunck
FOES: Zane and the ninja
SKILLS: Mind control
GEAR: Vermillion ax, Vermillion sword

KEY SET: Vermillion Invader
SET NUMBER: 70624
YEAR: 2017

ON TRACK

Raggmunk shares his Vermillion Invader tank with Slackjaw. It boasts separate cockpits for the two of them, a go-anywhere caterpillar track, and a pair of catapults for firing giant Vermillion eggs at their enemies!

RAGGMUNK SHARES HIS name with a tasty kind of pancake, but there's nothing sweet or savory about him! Despite his high status in the Vermillion Army, he is just a blundering brute. Like Commander Blunck, he is scared of their superior, Machia, and desperate to prove himself worthy to her.

RIVETT

FAST AND STRONG

Same scary helmet as Raggmunk and Tannin

Vermillion sword has one smooth and one serrated edge

SNAKE SURPRISE

In The Vermillion Attack set, Rivett and Slackjaw guard a giant Vermillion egg. Inside its silver shell are several red snake elements, which can be made to burst out using a hidden exploding function.

NINJA FILE

LIKES: Guarding Time Blades
DISLIKES: Guarding giant eggs
FRIENDS: Machia
FOES: Kai, Nya, Samurai X
SKILLS: Weapons wiz
GEAR: Vermillion ax, Vermillion sword

KEY SET: The Vermillion Attack
SET NUMBER: 70621
YEAR: 2017

DID YOU KNOW?

The Vermillions' eggs were laid long ago by one of the ninja's oldest enemies—the Great Devourer.

PRESENT THIS WARRIOR with any weapon, and she'll show instant expertise with it. Clever, quick, and acrobatic, she can tackle several enemies at once, even multiple ninja! Because Rivett is smarter than her superiors, Blunck and Raggmunk, she is often assigned missions directly by General Machia.

VERMILLION TROOPS

FANGED FIGHTERS

> Rattlesnake tail under eye shows his face is made from serpents!

> Upper set of fangs show on this side of dual face print

NINJA FILE

NAME: Slackjaw
KEY SET: The Vermillion Attack
SET NUMBER: 70621
YEAR: 2017

> Double-bladed Vermillion ax

> All Vermillion minifigures have detailed armor printing on their legs

> Lower fangs are projected on this side of dual face print

NINJA FILE

NAME: Vermin
KEY SET: Destiny's Shadow
SET NUMBER: 70623
YEAR: 2017

NINJA FILE

NAME: Tannin
KEY SET: Desert Lightning
SET NUMBER: 70622
YEAR: 2017

> "Hands of Time" emblem shows loyalty to the Time Twins

THESE FOOT SOLDIERS may look similar, but no two are the same. Slackjaw is a stickler for the rules. He's always trying to advance his career. Tannin can absorb almost any blow, as if he was made from rubber. Vermin is genetically modified, giving him excellent eyesight and hearing.

FUSION KAI

FIRE HEATS WATER

Eyes aflame with newfound Fusion power

NINJA FILE

LIKES: Finding his parents
DISLIKES: Fearing that his parents were traitors
FRIENDS: His sister, Nya
FOES: Raggmunk and Slackjaw
SKILLS: Fusing his elemental power with Nya's
GEAR: Dragon Dagger

KEY SET: Dragon's Forge
SET NUMBER: 70627
YEAR: 2017

TIME FOR A CHANGE

In The Vermillion Attack (set 70621), Kai wears the same gi, but with only a half-mask and no shoulder armor. Behind the half-mask, his mouth is set in a scowl rather than a smile, with no alternative golden eyes.

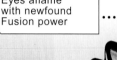

Belt harness includes a utility pouch and a Fire symbol on the buckle

REUNITED WITH HIS PARENTS after many years, Kai learns the true purpose of his father's Dragon Dagger. When used jointly by the Elemental Masters of Fire and Water, it can blend their mighty powers to summon the two-headed Fusion Dragon! Together, Kai and Nya ride the creature to the Boiling Sea.

DID YOU KNOW?

This minifigure is the first to show Kai with gold eyes on a standard yellow head rather than a red one.

FUSION NYA
WATER COOLS FIRE

NINJA FILE

LIKES: Finding her parents
DISLIKES: Seeing her family argue
FRIENDS: Her brother, Kai
FOES: The Buffmillion
SKILLS: Fusing her elemental power with Kai's
GEAR: Reversal Time Blade

KEY SET: Dragon's Forge
SET NUMBER: 70627
YEAR: 2017

Alternative expression shows standard black eyes and a smile

DID YOU KNOW?
Nya's parents were the first pair to ride the Fusion Dragon, using it to hide the Reversal Blade in the Boiling Sea.

Elemental water symbol on belt buckle

TWO HEADS ARE BETTER THAN ONE
In the Dragon's Forge set, Nya and Kai's Fusion Dragon has two heads with snapping jaws and a firing crossbow mounted on its back. It represents the combined Fire and Water abilities of the siblings' elemental powers.

Traditional zōri sandals fit between toes

AS THE COOLER HEAD in their elemental fusion, Nya helps Kai come to terms with the shocking news that their parents are alive. She is delighted to see them, while Kai is initially distrustful. When the siblings summon the Fusion Dragon, they use it to find the Reversal Time Blade.

FUSION LLOYD
MAKESHIFT MASTER

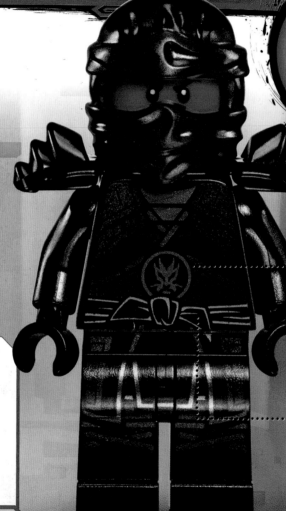

NINJA FILE

LIKES: The idea of being a dojo master
DISLIKES: The reality of filling Master Wu's sandals
FRIENDS: Jay
FOES: The Time Twins
SKILLS: Leadership
GEAR: Katanas

KEY SET: Dawn of Iron Doom
SET NUMBER: 70626
YEAR: 2017

DID YOU KNOW?
The Time Twins' Iron Doom mech is brought to life by Vermillion snakes slithering around its insides!

Dragon's head is Lloyd's personal elemental symbol

A WEIGHT OFF HIS SHOULDERS
In Destiny's Shadow (set 70623), Lloyd wears the same outfit, but without shoulder armor. That makes him all the more aerodynamic when he speeds his flying boat through the swamplands in pursuit of the Vermillion.

Belt knot worn centrally, unlike other ninja, who tie their belts on one side

WITH WU A PRISONER of the Time Twins, Lloyd steps up to become the ninja's new Master-in-training. With Jay at his side, he infiltrates the swamp fort where Krux and Acronix are holding Wu. To his surprise, he finds the Time Twins firing up their time-traveling mech, the enormous Iron Doom!

FUSION NINJA

TIME IS NOT ON THEIR SIDE!

NINJA FILE

NAME: Fusion Zane
SET NAME: Vermillion Invader
SET NUMBER: 70624
YEAR: 2017

Green facial scar reminds Cole of when he was a ghost

A practical length of climbing rope serves as Cole's belt

NINJA FILE

NAME: Fusion Cole
SET NAME: Destiny's Shadow
SET NUMBER: 70623
YEAR: 2017

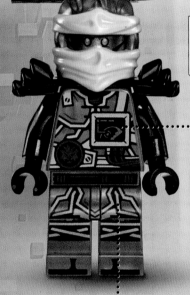

Radar scanner screen plugs into Zane's internal power source

NINJA FILE

NAME: Fusion Jay
SET NAME: Dawn of Iron Doom
SET NUMBER: 70626
YEAR: 2017

Outfit design is a darker shade of blue than on most other Jay minifigures

Printed robes and armor are more angular than those of the other ninja

THE NINJA LOOK STEALTHIER than ever when they take on the Time Twins and their Vermillion Army. Wearing muted shades of their familiar colors, Zane, Cole, and Jay are ready to follow Master Lloyd's instructions, while Nya and Kai are away looking for the truth about their parents.

Lightning emblem centered on a printed chest armor plate

RAY
DISAPPEARED DAD

Spiky, flame-shaped hair is similar to Kai's

Kindly smile has survived many years of hardship

Gold-trimmed blacksmith's apron reaches down to Ray's knees

NINJA FILE

LIKES: Making things
DISLIKES: Making things for the Vermillion
FRIENDS: Maya, Nya, Kai
FOES: Krux, Buffmillion
SKILLS: Master blacksmith
GEAR: Hot hammer and anvil

KEY SET: Dragon's Forge
SET NUMBER: 70627
YEAR: 2017

STUCK IN THE SWAMPS
Ray and Maya went missing when Kai and Nya were very young. With Krux threatening to harm their children, the former Elemental Masters had no choice but to become his prisoners, confined to an isolated blacksmith's forge in the swamplands.

DID YOU KNOW?
Ray stamped all the Vermillion's armor with his own mark, hoping to let his children know he was still alive.

RAY IS A BLACKSMITH and the former Elemental Master of Fire. He is also Kai and Nya's father. Forty years ago, he and his wife, Maya, made the Time Blades that helped Wu defeat Krux and Acronix. Now they are prisoners of Krux, forced to make armor for the Vermillion Army.

MAYA
MISSING MOM

Long hair flows like water (and covers a second alarmed expression!)

Heavy-duty gloves allow blacksmiths to hold and work with hot metal

DID YOU KNOW?
Nya grew up with no idea that her mom had gifted her the elemental powers of a Water Master.

SERVANTS OF SERPENTS
When Kai and Nya track down their parents, Kai thinks they must be willingly helping the Vermillion. In truth, they have been made to work under the eight watchful eyes of a four-headed Buffmillion monster!

NINJA FILE

LIKES: Her children
DISLIKES: Kai's suspicions
FRIENDS: Ray, Nya, Kai
FOES: Krux, Buffmillion
SKILLS: Blacksmith and peacemaker
GEAR: Cold hammer and anvil

KEY SET: Dragon's Forge
SET NUMBER: 70627
YEAR: 2017

KAI AND NYA'S MOM was once the Elemental Master of Water. Like her husband, Ray, she gave up her powers to focus on running their blacksmith's shop and raising their children. After years as a prisoner of Krux, she couldn't be happier when she finally sees her kids again.

NINJA VS. SONS OF GARMADON

RESISTANCE LLOYD
SON OF GARMADON

NINJA FILE

LIKES: Princess Harumi
DISLIKES: Biker gangs using his family name
FRIENDS: Nya
FOES: Ultra Violet
SKILLS: Stunt driving
GEAR: Dao, katanas

KEY SET: Ninja Nightcrawler
SET NUMBER: 70641
YEAR: 2018

Lloyd has green eyes for the first time in standard LEGO® NINJAGO® sets

Lloyd's new weapon is a dao, also known as a broadsword

Lime green detail on robes is new for Lloyd

DID YOU KNOW?
All the ninja got updated looks in 2018, incorporating design elements from THE LEGO® NINJAGO® MOVIE™.

GREEN STREAK
Lloyd's Ninja Nightcrawler is no ordinary racecar. It can switch between speed and attack modes, with a new kind of foldout rapid-fire shooters. It's ideal for keeping pace with Ultra Violet on the streets of Ninjago City.

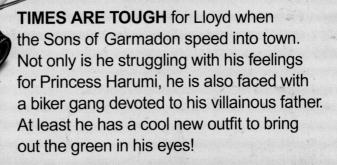

TIMES ARE TOUGH for Lloyd when the Sons of Garmadon speed into town. Not only is he struggling with his feelings for Princess Harumi, he is also faced with a biker gang devoted to his villainous father. At least he has a cool new outfit to bring out the green in his eyes!

SNAKE JAGUAR

SHH! IT'S REALLY ZANE!

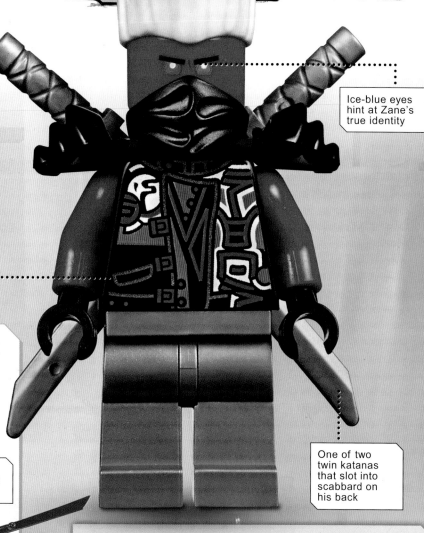

Ice-blue eyes hint at Zane's true identity

Same biker's vest worn by Skip Vicious and Luke Cunningham

HOLO PURSUIT

Zane drops his holographic disguise when his true identity is found out. Unfortunately, he's in the middle of the Street Race of Snake Jaguar (set 70639), proving his motorbike skills to Mr. E at the time!

Zane uses a bow and arrow in this set

One of two twin katanas that slot into scabbard on his back

THE TITANIUM NINJA'S latest upgrade lets him disguise himself with a hologram. He uses this ability to pose as bad-boy biker "Snake Jaguar" and goes undercover with the Sons of Garmadon. If his new "friends" find out that he's really a ninja, they'll be sure to scramble his circuits!

Helmet has a more ornate crest than on previous Samurai X minifigures

Curved shoulder armor in gold

NINJA FILE

LIKES: Being the newest member of the ninja team
DISLIKES: Being hacked
FRIENDS: Zane
FOES: Killow and "The Quiet One"
SKILLS: Superfast processing speeds
GEAR: Golden katanas

KEY SET: Killow vs. Samurai X
SET NUMBER: 70642
YEAR: 2018

X VS. VERMILLION

P.I.X.A.L. first assumes the mantle of Samurai X during the battle against the Vermillion. In 2017's Samurai VXL (set 70625), P.I.X.A.L. wears blue armor and fights alongside Nya, the original Samurai X.

Red stripes on armor recall Samurai X's early look

WHEN NYA STOPS using her Samurai X identity, P.I.X.A.L. uploads her artificial intelligence to the Samurai X suit. At first, the ninja are suspicious of the new hero on the scene, but when they learn that it is their android friend, they are pleased to have her on the team.

DID YOU KNOW?

P.I.X.A.L. lost her original body during the Tournament of Elements and lived inside Zane's head for a while.

RESISTANCE COLE
FATHER FIGURE

NINJA FILE

LIKES: Seeing Wu grow up
DISLIKES: Diapers
FRIENDS: Baby Wu
FOES: Chopper Maroon and "The Quiet One"
SKILLS: Babysitting
GEAR: Giant hammer, katanas

KEY SET: Temple of Resurrection
SET NUMBER: 70643
YEAR: 2018

New-style ninja wrap made from two pieces so top half can be swapped for hair

Single-shoulder armor includes a scabbard at the back

Symbols spell Cole's element, "EARTH," in Ninjago language

BABY WU
When Cole rescues a baby from the Sons of Garmadon, he doesn't realize that it is Master Wu, turned back into a newborn by the Reversal Time Blade. Cole considers calling him "Cole Junior" until he discovers the truth!

DID YOU KNOW?
Temple of Resurrection is the largest Sons of Garmadon set, with a whopping 765 pieces.

IN HIS NEW-LOOK no-nonsense gi, Cole leads the search for the missing Master Wu. Rock-steady Cole is more serious than ever. When he discovers that Wu has been transformed into a baby, he is determined to act as his guardian and protector, carrying his former master on his back.

RESISTANCE NINJA
GOING FOR GARMADON

Jay's minifigure now has visible freckles

Symbol for "W" in Ninjago language stands for "water"

NINJA FILE

NAME: Resistance Jay
KEY SET: Killow vs. Samurai X
SET NUMBER: 70642
YEAR: 2018

New fabric piece depicts samurai kusazuri armor

Utility pouches make up for lack of gi pockets!

Determined frown can be switched to an embarrassed grin

Diamond printing depicts the weave of Kai's gi

NINJA FILE

NAME: Resistance Kai
KEY SET: Katana V11
SET NUMBER: 70638
YEAR: 2018

NINJA FILE

NAME: Resistance Nya
KEY SET: Ninja Nightcrawler
SET NUMBER: 70641
YEAR: 2018

THE LAST LINE of resistance against the return of Garmadon, the ninja crew needs to be better equipped than ever. Each fighter wears a high-tech weave, with armor on their left shoulder. The right shoulder of each ninja is left unencumbered for easy access to twin katanas.

DID YOU KNOW?

All six team members wear an eight-sided ninja symbol on their backs in the Sons of Garmadon sets.

PRINCESS HARUMI

A ROYAL PAIN

SECRET SCHEME

Harumi's ultimate plan is to resurrect Lord Garmadon using three ancient Oni Masks. When the masks are brought together, they can open a door between the living world and the Departed Realm!

Lotus flower design on large ceremonial cape

Royal robes accessorized with gold slippers

AS A CHILD, Harumi lost her parents in the destruction caused by one of the ninja team's many battles. She was then adopted by the Emperor and Empress of Ninjago, becoming a princess overnight. Now she pretends to be a fan of the ninja while secretly plotting revenge against them.

DID YOU KNOW?

Princess Harumi is also known as Rumi, the Jade Princess, and, to a select few, "The Quiet One"!

No other character has this hair piece in white

Red katanas are the signature weapon for the Sons of Garmadon gang

DID YOU KNOW?

Harumi uses the codename "Quiet One" because she barely spoke after losing her parents as a child.

STONE SERVANT

In Oni Titan (set 70658), Harumi has revived Garmadon in his most monstrous form and is helping him lay waste to Ninjago City. However, most of the work is being done by a stone giant, also known as the Colossus!

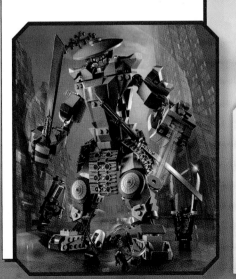

NINJA FILE

LIKES: Chaos
DISLIKES: Her royal parents
FRIENDS: The S.O.G.
FOES: Lloyd and the ninja
SKILLS: Ruthlessness
GEAR: Red katana

KEY SET: Throne Room Showdown
SET NUMBER: 70651
YEAR: 2018

When she's not pretending to be a perfect princess, Harumi secretly leads the Sons of Garmadon! The S.O.G have no idea who they are working for and call her simply "The Quiet One." Lloyd is very upset when he finds out the truth, because he is in love with Harumi.

HUTCHINS

PALACE PROTECTOR

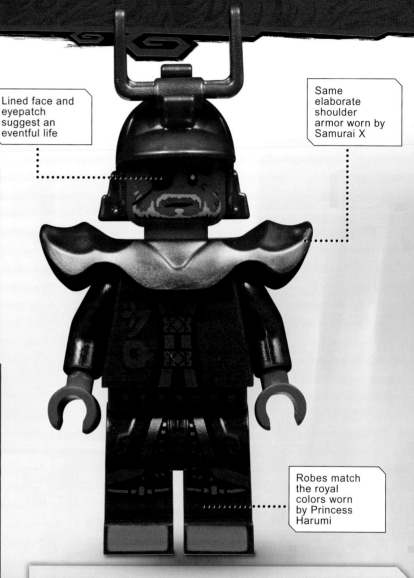

NINJA FILE

LIKES: His duties
DISLIKES: Seeing Harumi unhappy
FRIENDS: The Emperor and Empress of Ninjago
FOES: Traitors to Ninjago
SKILLS: Manners and martial arts
GEAR: Ceremonial staff

KEY SET: Temple of Resurrection
SET NUMBER: 70643
YEAR: 2018

Lined face and eyepatch suggest an eventful life

Robes match the royal colors worn by Princess Harumi

SURLY TEMPLE
When Harumi uses the Temple of Resurrection to summon Lord Garmadon from the Departed Realm, Hutchins is distraught to see one of his beloved palace buildings take on the appearance of a monstrous face!

WHEN THE SONS OF GARMADON attack the royal palace, the ninja suspect Hutchins of helping the gang. In fact, this long-time servant of the Ninjago royal family is as loyal as they come. He doesn't find it easy to express his feelings, but his heart is always in the right place.

MR. E
ENIGMATIC ENEMY

Red-tinted visor
adds to Mr. E's
air of menace

DID YOU KNOW?
One of the only
things the ninja find
out about Mr. E is that
he is a Nindroid,
just like Zane.

"G" for "Garmadon"
is among the
badges and patches
on leather jacket

Pants have zip-up
pockets so items
can't fly out when
traveling at speed

MASK OF VENGEANCE
The Oni Mask of Vengeance was
kept in a secret compartment in Borg
Tower until it was stolen by the Sons
of Garmadon. When Mr. E puts it on,
he gains two more arms and the
ability to absorb others' powers!

EVEN HIS FELLOW Sons of Garmadon
don't know much about Mr. E. Behind his
tinted helmet is an even more mysterious
mask. There's no point asking what his
initial stands for, as Mr. E never speaks.
He lets his swords do the talking—
especially when the ninja want to chat!

ULTRA VIOLET

UNPREDICTABLE FORCE

When not worn in a high ponytail like this, Ultra Violet puts her hair in pigtails

Facial tattoos would make Ultra Violet unmistakable in a police line-up!

Bike chain hangs from studded belt for a heavy-metal look

MASK OF HATRED

The Sons of Garmadon take the Oni Mask of Hatred after Lloyd and Harumi find it in a temple deep in the jungle. When Ultra Violet wears it, it encases her body in fiery stone armor, making her invincible!

THERE'S NO WAY TO KNOW what this wild villain will do next. She's always looking for the next big thrill and doesn't care how dangerous it is. She laughs at the strangest (and cruelest) things but is almost always in a bad mood. She certainly belongs in the Sons of Garmadon!

KILLOW
S.O.G.'S BIGGEST BIKER

Bearded face hidden by Oni Mask of Deception

His name is tattooed on his belly—in case he forgets it!

NINJA FILE

LIKES: Working out
DISLIKES: Small parking spaces
FRIENDS: Ultra Violet
FOES: Jay, Samurai X
SKILLS: Skateboarding (one board for each foot)
GEAR: Huge spiked club

KEY SET: Killow vs. Samurai X
SET NUMBER: 70642
YEAR: 2018

MASK OF DECEPTION
The Sons of Garmadon steal the Oni Mask of Deception from the Ninjago Royal Palace. Wearing it lets Killow move objects with his mind—though he prefers to scatter things in all directions with his giant circular-saw-wheel bike!

KILLOW IS A RECRUITER for the Sons of Garmadon. He tests all potential gang members in a road race where rules and fairness take a back seat. Killow has decorated his vest and his skin with S.O.G. symbols. An Oni Mask is the final menacing touch.

Nothing says "Garmadon gang member" like a pair of skull-shaped kneepads!

CHOPPER MAROON

RALLYING REDHEAD

Black makeup around eyes makes them look like sunken pits!

Bandana mask can be worn with knot at front to show full face

Torso print shows one sew-on skull patch and one spray-painted design

NINJA FILE

LIKES: Skulls
DISLIKES: Feeling the wind in his hair
FRIENDS: Mr. E, Nails
FOES: Lloyd, Cole
SKILLS: Swordplay and motorcycle mechanics
GEAR: Katana and wrench

KEY SET: Temple of Resurrection
SET NUMBER: 70643
YEAR: 2018

CHOPPERS LOCKS

Chopper's hair piece, which continues down the back of his head, was created for a LEGO® DIMENSIONS minifigure in 2016. The Sons of Garmadon are the first to wear it in red. Both Chopper and Nails sport the same distinctive cut.

DID YOU KNOW?

A "chopper" motorcycle is one made from parts chopped up from other bikes to create a dramatic new look.

WITH HIS FACE PAINTED like a skull and his hair cropped into a bold red mohawk, Chopper is determined to be the scariest Son of Garmadon he can be. Sure, wearing a mask slightly undermines the skull effect, but the two extra skulls on his biker jacket help get the point across.

S.O.G. GANG MEMBERS

GAGA FOR GARMADON

Flip-down eyepieces for close-up engine repair work

DID YOU KNOW?

The Sons of Garmadon have their secret headquarters in a disused Ninjago City subway station.

Same brightly colored jacket worn by Skip Vicious

Four silver studs worn on forehead

NINJA FILE

NAME: Luke Cunningham
KEY SET: Katana V11
SET NUMBER: 70638
YEAR: 2018

NINJA FILE

NAME: Nails
KEY SET: S.O.G. Headquarters
SET NUMBER: 70640
YEAR: 2018

Skip hasn't shaved—that would mean taking his helmet off!

NINJA FILE

NAME: Skip Vicious
KEY SET: S.O.G. Headquarters
SET NUMBER: 70640
YEAR: 2018

Nails is the only S.O.G. minifigure to have short legs

Bare arms and biker gloves is the standard S.O.G. look.

THESE MOTLEY S.O.G. are the foot soldiers of their biker gang—though they don't like going anywhere on foot. Luke Cunningham and Skip Vicious are often mistaken for each other, but as they are constantly pointing out to people, their helmets have completely different visors!

DID YOU KNOW?

In her day job, Skylor runs the chain of noodle restaurants set up by her father, Master Chen.

Gritted teeth can be switched to a relaxed look

NINJA FILE

LIKES: Giving her frie~~~ free noodles
DISLIKES: That she might never see Kai again
FRIENDS: Lloyd, Nya
FOES: Harumi
SKILLS: Power absorption
GEAR: Katanas and shurikens

KEY SET: Throne Room Showdown
SET NUMBER: 70651
YEAR: 2018

THE THREE MASTERS

In a 2017 minifigure pack (set 853687), Skylor wears a hood and wields a bow. She makes up a trio of Elemental Masters alongside Shade, the Master of Shadows, and Ash, the Master of Smoke.

Belt piece clips between legs and torso

Spare sword can be carried on her back

MANY ALLIES OF THE NINJA come to the aid of the city when Harumi and the Sons of Garmadon seize control of Ninjago! As the Master of Amber, Skylor dons a new costume to team up with Lloyd and Nya. Meanwhile, the other four ninja are trapped in a different Realm.

EMPEROR GARMADON

EVEN MORE POWERFUL!

One-piece helmet designed for THE LEGO NINJAGO MOVIE

One of two giant naginata spears

DID YOU KNOW?

When he becomes Emperor, Garmadon bans all green things—because it is Lloyd's elemental color!

Purple ooze spills from Garmadon's cracked armor

NINJA FILE

LIKES: Destruction
DISLIKES: Green
FRIENDS: Harumi
FOES: The ninja
SKILLS: Conjuring giant stone monsters
GEAR: Katanas, naginata spears

KEY SET: Temple of Resurrection
SET NUMBER: 70643
YEAR: 2018

GARMADON TRIUMPHANT

When Harumi revives Garmadon at the Temple of Resurrection, she unleashes a chain of terrible events. Cole, Jay, Kai, Zane, and Wu are all seemingly destroyed, leaving Lloyd and Nya as the last two ninja.

THOUGHT GARMADON was bad before? Meet this version! No trace of good remains—only a passion to destroy. With Harumi and the Sons of Garmadon ready to obey his orders, nothing can stop him from becoming Emperor Garmadon!

145

SPINJITZU MASTER KAI

ROLLING FIRE

Top part of headwrap has colors reversed from main S.O.G. variant

Lower part of headwrap is unchanged from other S.O.G. sets

NINJA FILE

LIKES: Doing the Leapfrog
DISLIKES: Losing balance
FRIENDS: His fellow Spinjitzu Masters
FOES: The S.O.G.
SKILLS: Getting in a spin
GEAR: Dragon swords and shurikens

KET SET: Kai—Spinjitzu Master
SET NUMBER: 70633
YEAR: 2018

A FRESH SPIN

Each Spinjitzu Masters set features a handheld spinner, complete with a ripcord and brick-built grip. When the ripcord is pulled, the spinner rolls, spins, or jumps away. Ninja, go!

Elemental Fire energy bursts from Kai's lightweight training gi

AS A SPINJITZU MASTER, Kai can turn up the heat on his opponents by spinning in a blur of elemental Fire energy! His robes are emblaoned with flames so that everyone knows his Spinjitzu moves—such as the Orbit, the Zen, the Leapfrog, and the Palm Spin— are simply too hot to handle.

SPINJITZU MASTER NYA

ROLLING WAVE

From 2018, standard Nya minifigures all have a mole on one cheek

Waves and splashes represent Nya's element, water

BONUS BUILD
Each Spinjitzu Masters set comes with a pair of minifigure shurikens and a buildable weapons rack for storing other gear. In Nya's case, the rack has room for a spear and a water feature!

All six Spinjitzu Masters minifigures share this leg print

NINJA FILE

LIKES: Doing the Zen
DISLIKES: Getting dizzy
FRIENDS: The other Spinjitzu Masters
FOES: The S.O.G.
SKILLS: Making a splash
GEAR: Spear and shurikens

KEY SET: Nya—Spinjitzu Master
SET NUMBER: 70634
YEAR: 2018

NYA'S SIMPLE BLACK training outfit gets a splash of color when she activates her Spinjitzu powers. Wave energy washes over her, and she becomes a whirlpool of martial arts moves. Any foe that gets in her way will feel like they've just been washed down a very big drain!

DID YOU KNOW?
Perfecting the Zen move requires spinning the ninja to hover for a time in the air—like Wu does when he meditates.

SPINJITZU MASTER JAY

ROLLING THUNDER

Blue bolts of lightning energy crackle across Jay's training robes

NEW GIS IN A POD
Jay wears training robes without elemental enhancement in his Kendo Training Pod (set 853758). The same gis are also worn by Lloyd and Cole in their own portable training pod sets.

Same leg print shared by Jay's Kendo Training Pod minifigure

DID YOU KNOW?
The LEGO NINJAGO website includes videos with tips for getting the most from your spinner.

AS A SPINJITZU MASTER, Jay can turn like a wheel until he is moving so fast, he becomes a blur! This allows him to perform amazing Spinjitzu moves, including his favorite, the Drift. His body buzzes with elemental lightning energy, telling his enemies to stay away or get zapped!

NINJA FILE

NAME: Spinjitzu Master Lloyd
KEY SET: S.O.G. Headquarters
SET NUMBER: 70640
YEAR: 2018

Lloyd's elemental energy flows from his heart

Focused, robotic stare

Hands match color detail on headwrap and robes

Zane's elemental power has even iced up his belt!

Earth powers turn Cole's gi to rock and lava!

NINJA FILE

NAME: Spinjitzu Master Cole
KEY SET: Cole—Spinjitzu Master
SET NUMBER: 70637
YEAR: 2018

NINJA FILE

NAME: Spinjitzu Master Zane
KEY SET: Zane—Spinjitzu Master
SET NUMBER: 70636
YEAR: 2018

Cole is the only Spinjitzu Masters minifigure to have bare arms

EACH OF THE NINJA practices Spinjitzu in their own unique way—the results of which are evident from their elementally enhanced clothes! Once they start spinning, each ninja's robes are a blur, but they can be distinguished by the color of their unique energy tornadoes!

COLE, KAI, JAY, AND ZANE are a long way from home when they face the Iron Baron and his Dragon Hunters in the Realm of Oni and Dragons. Meanwhile, Lloyd and Nya are still in Ninjago City facing big troubles of their own!

WHOEVER CAME UP WITH THIS STORY DESERVES A BIG HAND!

CHAPTER TEN

NINJA VS. DRAGON HUNTERS

HUNTED LLOYD
RAGGED RESISTANCE FIGHTER

Faded "Wu-Cru" logo is a stylized image of Master Wu

NINJA FILE

LIKES: Recruiting a resistance force
DISLIKES: Giving up hope
FRIENDS: The resistance
FOES: Emperor Garmadon
SKILLS: Leadership
GEAR: Sword and sashimono

KEY SET: Oni Titan
SET NUMBER: 70658
YEAR: 2018

DID YOU KNOW?

Lloyd appears in a set with the Oni Titan. This LEGO giant is more than 9 inches (25 cm) high. That's six times taller than a minifigure!

Metal of battle-damaged armor shows where green paint has chipped off

Torn and tattered belt has seen better days

FLYING THE FLAG

When Lloyd goes into battle against the Oni Titan, he wears a sashimono on his back. This tall, thin banner is a traditional samurai accessory, and makes it easier for Nya to see Lloyd as they work together in battle.

LEGO® sashimono made from bar and clip pieces

IT'S NO WONDER that Lloyd looks angry. He has lost his elemental power, his father is in charge of Ninjago City, and he and Nya seem to be the only two ninja left. Hunted by Emperor Garmadon's followers, Lloyd's urban street gi is put together from whatever useful equipment he can salvage.

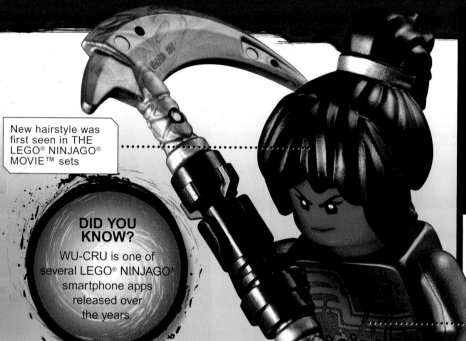

New hairstyle was first seen in THE LEGO® NINJAGO® MOVIE™ sets

NINJA FILE

LIKES: Staying cool in a crisis
DISLIKES: Her brother, Kai, going missing
FRIENDS: Lloyd
FOES: The Oni Titan
SKILLS: Engineering
GEAR: Double-bladed scythe

KEY SET: Oni Titan
SET NUMBER: 70658
YEAR: 2018

DID YOU KNOW?

WU-CRU is one of several LEGO® NINJAGO® smartphone apps released over the years.

CRU OF TWO

In Wu-Cru Target Training (set 30530), Nya and Lloyd prepare for battle without their usual team. Both ninja wear white training robes with gold Master Wu logos, and Nya still has her old hairstyle.

Blue stripes and Wu-Cru logo starting to deteriorate on well-worn top

Scythe is just one of the weapons Nya has designed

NYA KNOWS THAT THINGS LOOK BLEAK with Emperor Garmadon in control of Ninjago City and most of the ninja team missing. But this Master of Water doesn't have time for tears! She is busy crafting weapons and gear to keep herself and Lloyd one step ahead of the Sons of Garmadon.

HUNTED NINJA

LOST IN ANOTHER REALM

NINJA FILE

NAME: Hunted Kai
KEY SET: Destiny's Wing
SET NUMBER: 70650
YEAR: 2018

Shoulder armor for the harsh new environment

One bare arm after Kai's sleeve was torn off in an accident

NINJA FILE

NAME: Hunted Jay
KEY SET: Stormbringer
SET NUMBER: 70652
YEAR: 2018

Each outfit is a ripped version of the ones worn to fight the Sons of Garmadon

Headwrap remains undamaged

DID YOU KNOW?

The Realm of Oni and Dragons is the oldest of the 16 Realms, and was once home to Master Wu's father.

NINJA FILE

NAME: Hunted Cole
KEY SET: Firstbourne
SET NUMBER: 70653
YEAR: 2018

Kai's new makeshift armor is printed on his torso and legs

MOST OF THE NINJA TEAM are forced to transport themselves out of the Ninjago Realm after the Oni Titan crushes the *Destiny's Bounty* with them onboard! They land in the Realm of Oni and Dragons. It's a harsh place, and the ninja's robes quickly tatter as they search for a way home.

Chest scratched and gi slashed open following an encounter with a dragon

HUNTED ZANE
WANTED FOR SCRAP

Valuable titanium arm exposed by damage to robes

Chunky carved hilt helps balance the weight of the sword

THE WAY BACK

To get back to Ninjago City, the ninja must find all four pieces of the fabled Dragon Armor. In the Stormbringer set, Zane and Jay already have the armor's Dragonbone Blade and are battling for possession of the golden Dragon Chestplate.

IN THE REALM OF ONI AND DRAGONS, Zane is faced with his own special danger. Hard-bitten Dragon Hunters roam the land, looking for scrap metal to use in their dirty dragon-hunting work. As Zane is made from top-notch titanium, the hunters would love to catch him and cannibalize his parts!

IRON BARON

LEADER OF THE DRAGON HUNTERS

NINJA FILE

LIKES: Ruling his gang with an iron fist
DISLIKES: Dragons
FRIENDS: Heavy Metal
FOES: Wu and the ninja
SKILLS: Cunning, deceit
GEAR: Cyborg arm, tanto sword, and horned staff

KEY SET: Dieselnaut
SET NUMBER: 70654
YEAR: 2018

DID YOU KNOW?

The Iron Baron's false leg, cyborg arm, and scarred face are a result of encounters with dragons.

Slot for a short tanto sword worn across the chest

Cyborg arm piece clips on to a standard minifigure hand

MONSTER TRUCK

The Iron Baron's Dieselnaut is a powerful, air-polluting tank that reflects his disregard for the environment. The other Dragon Hunters are happy to travel on it until the ninja teach them to respect their fellow creatures.

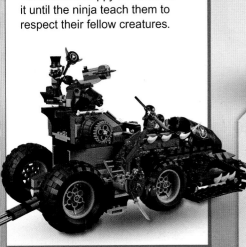

WITHOUT THE IRON BARON, the Dragon Hunters might be a very different group. Driven by a deep loathing of dragons and a lust for power, he has tricked his followers into a miserable existence based on fear and lies. His ultimate goal is to collect the Dragon Armor pieces before the ninja.

HEAVY METAL

AN ACT OF FAITH

Broad hat helps disguise Faith's features, as well as keeping the sun off!

Same shoulder armor as the Iron Baron, but worn the other way around

Printed D-clip on belt for hanging from the HunterCopter

HUNTING PARTY

In the Firstbourne set, Heavy Metal goes dragon hunting alongside Chew Toy, Jet Jack, and Muzzle. Muzzle wears the same armor and mask as Heavy Metal but has a different face print and a hood instead of a hat.

Muzzle has two red eyes behind his mask

THE IRON BARON'S RIGHT-HAND MAN isn't the person he believes them to be. Heavy Metal is a name and disguise adopted by an idealistic woman named Faith. She is as full of faith as her name suggests and hopes for a better future for her Realm. If she were in charge, she would run things very differently ….

DADDY NO LEGS

ALSO KNOWN AS DADDY NEW LEGS!

NINJA FILE

LIKES: Never getting socks as a gift

DISLIKES: His inaccurate nickname

FRIENDS: The Iron Baron

FOES: Stormbringer

SKILLS: Tracking

GEAR: Vengestone chain, sword

KEY SET: Stormbringer
SET NUMBER: 70652
YEAR: 2018

Same top-tied hairstyle as Nadakhan the Sky Pirate captain

CHAIN OF CALAMITIES

Daddy No Legs' cyborg body isn't just for getting around. It also features a built-in chain weapon for grabbing onto dragons such as Stormbringer and then bringing the poor creatures back to the Dragon Hunters' base.

Mechanical lower body made from 23 LEGO elements

DID YOU KNOW?

The Dragon Hunters use Vengestone weapons because they block the elemental powers of their prey.

YEARS AGO, this determined Dragon Hunter lost his legs in a skirmish with his intended target. Now he gets around on a set of four mechanical limbs and is faster and more agile than ever before! Alongside Heavy Metal, he is one of the Iron Baron's most celebrated hunter-generals.

Gauge displays the runtime left in these speedy robot legs

NINJA FILE

LIKES: Overlooking everyone on the ground
DISLIKES: Being overlooked by her boss
FRIENDS: The hunters
FOES: Kai and Cole
SKILLS: Dragon herding
GEAR: Jetpack, spear, kaginawa blade

KEY SET: Destiny's Wing
SET NUMBER: 70650
YEAR: 2018

Jet Jack's aerial acrobatics are enough to make her hair stand on end!

Both jetpack straps are chained securely across Jack's chest

Jetpack wings can be tilted up and down and angled at the tips

FIGHT AND FLIGHT
The Destiny's Wing set sees Jack and her jetpack go up against Kai in his one-seater plane. Both are competing for one part of the Dragon Armor: the golden Dragonbone Blade!

AS AN AIRBORNE HUNTER, Jet Jack is responsible for scaring dragons out of the sky and onto the ground, where they are easier to catch. She wishes that the Iron Baron paid more attention to her work. She is a prime candidate to turn against him if a new leader ever emerges.

DRAGON HUNTERS
THE REST OF THE TRIBE

No other Dragon Hunter wears a welder's mask

NINJA FILE

NAME: Arkade
KEY SET: Dragon Pit
SET NUMBER: 70655
YEAR: 2018

DID YOU KNOW?
In both his set appearances, Chew Toy wields a turkey leg to lure hungry dragons toward him.

Samurai-style helmet crest is broken on one side

Ninja-style facemask distinguishes Skullbreaker from his friend Muzzle

Arkade makes decisions based on the spin of his built-in slot machine

Armor is slashed and battered from multiple dragon encounters

NINJA FILE

NAME: Skullbreaker
KEY SET: Dieselnaut
SET NUMBER: 70654
YEAR: 2018

Heavy-duty metal toecaps printed on front of feet

THE IRON BARON'S LOWER RANKS are an even odder bunch than his high-up hunters! Arkade gets his name from the slot machine in his armor; Chew Toy is so called because of his willingness to get close to dragons; and Skullbreaker … is probably just a traditional name in the Oni Realm!

NINJA FILE

NAME: Chew Toy
KEY SET: Firstbourne
SET NUMBER: 70653
YEAR: 2018

TEEN WU

PAST MASTER

Wu's minifigure wields a katana rather than a staff for the first time in the Dieselnaut set

NINJA FILE

LIKES: Relearning his own wisdom

DISLIKES: Lost memories

FRIENDS: The stranded ninja

FOES: Skullbreaker and Muzzle

SKILLS: Disguise

GEAR: Katana sword

KEY SET: Dieselnaut

SET NUMBER: 70654

YEAR: 2018

Wu's head hair is white even when he's a teenager!

Dragon Hunter disguise is a ploy to get inside the Iron Baron's base

STONE WARRIOR

The Dieselnaut set comes with all four parts of the Dragon Armor, as forged by Firstbourne and the First Spinjitzu Master. It can be worn by Wu or mounted on a buildable minifigure statue.

Plain gray minifigure body parts

WU HAS GROWN RAPIDLY since he returned to Ninjago as a baby. Now, in the Realm of Oni and Dragons, he is even beginning to get a beard again! His memories of who he is are also coming back, including the fact that his father was the First Spinjitzu Master.

DRAGON MASTER WU

GOLDEN NOT-SO-OLDIE!

NINJA FILE

LIKES: Dragons
DISLIKES: Dragon Hunters
FRIENDS: Firstbourne
FOES: Iron Baron
SKILLS: Empathy
GEAR: Golden Dragon Armor

KEY SET: Dragon Pit
SET NUMBER: 70655
YEAR: 2018

The Dragon Chestplate has studs on the back for attaching a flag

The large Dragon Shield depicts Firstbourne in flight

The Dragonbone Blade has a hilt shaped like a dragon's head

MASKED MASTER

Wu's minifigure wears a ninja mask for the first time ever in the spinner set Golden Dragon Master (set 70644). Behind the blingy bandana, he sports his black teenage mustache, stubble, and goatee beard.

ACCORDING TO LEGEND, whoever wears the First Spinjitzu Master's Dragon Armor will control the dragon Firstbourne. But when Wu dons the armor, he understands that it has no special powers. It was his father's love and respect for Firstbourne that allowed him to ride and work with the mighty creature.

DRAGON MASTER JAY

SPIN TO WING

NINJA FILE

LIKES: Spreading his wings
DISLIKES: Turbulence
FRIENDS: Dragon Masters
FOES: Low ceilings
SKILLS: Doing the Dragon Flip
GEAR: Shurikens

KEY SET: Jay—Dragon Master
SET NUMBER: 70646
YEAR: 2018

Focused stare can be swapped for a look of trepidation

Traditional ninja gi under pilot-style straps

LIGHTNING IN THE SKY

Each Dragon Masters set comes with a flying minifigure spinner and a hand-held launcher for performing ninja stunts such as the Dragon Strike, the Dragon Flip, the Eye of the Dragon, and the Nosediving Dragon!

DID YOU KNOW?

When they get back to Ninjago, the ninja use their newfound skills to defeat Emperor Garmadon.

Kneepads help ensure a soft landing after a spin in the air

JAY HELPS WU look on the bright side when they are lost in the Land of Oni and Dragons, and in return, Wu helps Jay summon his Elemental Dragon. In his Dragon Master gear, Jay looks like a cross between a ninja and a high-speed pilot, with ejector-seat straps and survival gear pockets.

DID YOU KNOW?

Lloyd and Nya do not have Dragon Master outfits, as they never visit the Realm of Oni and Dragons.

NINJA FILE

NAME: Dragon Master Zane
KEY SET: Zane—Dragon Master
SET NUMBER: 70648
YEAR: 2018

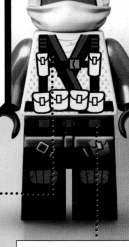

Kai wears a ragged scarf over his Dragon Master flying straps

Angular robe print reflects Zane's Nindroid identity

Pilot's belt packed full of survival gear in case of a crash-landing

NINJA FILE

NAME: Dragon Master Kai
KEY SET: Kai—Dragon Master
SET NUMBER: 70647
YEAR: 2018

Choice of hard stare or relaxed look

NINJA FILE

NAME: Dragon Master Cole
KEY SET: Cole—Dragon Master
SET NUMBER: 70645
YEAR: 2018

Same leg printing as Jay, Zane, and Cole

EACH OF THE STRANDED NINJA calls on their Elemental Dragon to escape the Oni Realm after Wu wins the trust of Firstbourne. Their Dragon Master robes appear exclusively in a range of five spinner sets, complete with large, foil dragon wings that help them take to the air!

Each Dragon Masters torso print includes a dragon symbol on their back

THE HEAT IS ON when the Serpentine Sorcerer Aspheera attacks Ninjago with her Pyro Vipers. But when the action moves into the frozen Never-Realm, the Ice Emperor and his Blizzard Samurai give the ninja a frosty reception!

BRRR! THIS CHAPTER EVEN GIVES ME THE CHILLS!

ASPHEERA
TWISTING FIRESTARTER

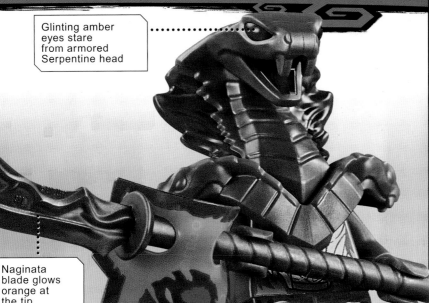

Glinting amber eyes stare from armored Serpentine head

Naginata blade glows orange at the tip

Scroll of Forbidden Spinjitzu can glow with fire power

NINJA FILE

LIKES: Burning Ninjago
DISLIKES: Being stuck in a pyramid for 1,000 years
FRIENDS: Char
FOES: Master Wu
SKILLS: Forbidden Spinjitzu, sorcery
GEAR: Scroll of Forbidden Spinjitzu

KEY SET: Fire Fang
SET NUMBER: 70674
YEAR: 2019

FLAME ON
Aspheera likes to arrive in a blaze of glory, so she travels on a throne of swords, on the back of Fire Fang's head! As if her golden armor wasn't showy enough to start with ....

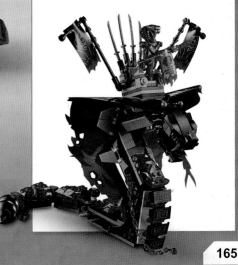

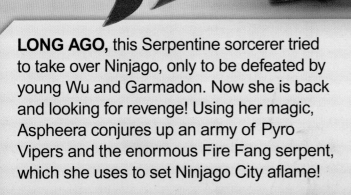

LONG AGO, this Serpentine sorcerer tried to take over Ninjago, only to be defeated by young Wu and Garmadon. Now she is back and looking for revenge! Using her magic, Aspheera conjures up an army of Pyro Vipers and the enormous Fire Fang serpent, which she uses to set Ninjago City aflame!

Scepter for guarding the Fire Scroll of Forbidden Spinjitzu

Fangs are still visible between closed jaws

NINJA FILE

LIKES: Imagining there's a spark between him and Aspheera
DISLIKES: When she gives him the cold shoulder
FRIENDS: The Pyro Vipers
FOES: The ninja
SKILLS: Giving and taking orders
GEAR: Snakes-head scepter

KEY SET: Katana 4X4
SET NUMBER: 70675
YEAR: 2019

DID YOU KNOW?
The symbols on Char's long belly spell out "FIRE" in the written language of Ninjago.

CHAR IN CHARGE
Char leads Pyro Whipper and Pyro Slayer into battle against Kai and Nya in the Katana 4X4 set. It's three against two, but the ninja have a new off-road car and Forbidden Spinjitzu powers on their side!

LIKE THE OTHER PYRO VIPERS, Char was a harmless Serpentine mummy in a museum until Aspheera came back to Ninjago! Now he has been fired into life by her sorcery and acts as her loyal servant. Little does Aspheera realize that Char is burning up with unrequited love for her ….

PYRO VIPERS

ASPHEERA'S SERPENTINE SQUAD

NINJA FILE

NAME: Pyro Slayer
KEY SET: Fire Fang
SET NUMBER: 70674
YEAR: 2019

Fire burns beneath charred bindings

The whip is a rare weapon in LEGO® NINJAGO® sets

Long-handled nagamaki sword

Chest armor has snake heads on both shoulders

Pyro Destroyer wields a curved blade with short handle

NINJA FILE

NAME: Pyro Destroyer
KEY SET: Cole's Dirt Bike
SET NUMBER: 70672
YEAR: 2019

NINJA FILE

NAME: Pyro Whipper
KEY SET: Katana 4X4
SET NUMBER: 70675
YEAR: 2019

Studded round shield new to LEGO NINJAGO sets in 2019

UNLIKE THEIR GENERAL, the average Pyro Viper is a mindless, obedient warrior with no free will of its own. Each one has been brought to life by Aspheera's fire magic and can be turned back into a lifeless museum mummy if its inner blaze is extinguished.

ARMOR KAI

POWERLESS

Ninja hood is a single piece again, unlike those the ninja wore in 2018

Sword slots into the back of Kai's new-look armor

NINJA FILE

LIKES: Rediscovering his True Potential
DISLIKES: Aspheera misusing his powers
FRIENDS: Powerful ninja
FOES: Aspheera
SKILLS: Burning rubber in the Katana 4X4
GEAR: Silver and gold katana swords

KEY SET: Katana 4X4
SET NUMBER: 70675
YEAR: 2019

POWERS BACK

Kai also appears in a 2019 Minifigure Pack (set 40342). The set includes the archaeologist Clutch Powers, who accidentally uncovers the prison that has held Aspheera for the last 1,000 years!

WHEN THE NINJA FACE ASPHEERA, she strips Kai of his elemental powers and adds them to her own. Can Kai still be a hero if he is no longer the Master of Fire? He has his doubts, but he soon learns that a ninja is defined by his choices, not his powers. And he still has a few sword skills to keep him safe!

ARMOR NINJA

SEARCHING FOR SCROLLS

Each ninja wears this new shoulder armor element

NINJA FILE

NAME: Armor Jay
KEY SET: Land Bounty
SET NUMBER: 70677
YEAR: 2019

Cole's hammer has a new dragon's head handle

Lightning and smiley face badges pinned to harness strap

NINJA FILE

NAME: Armor Cole
KEY SET: Cole's Dirt Bike
SET NUMBER: 70672
YEAR: 2019

NINJA FILE

NAME: Armor Nya
KEY SET: Land Bounty
SET NUMBER: 70677
YEAR: 2019

Each ninja's headband now features their initial

NEW ROBES MEAN a new start for the ninja, who have become somewhat lazy since their last great victory. But if they want to defeat Aspheera, they will need more than just a change of wardrobe. They must stop Aspheera from gaining the Scrolls of Forbidden Spinjitzu!

Missile to load into the Land Bounty's launcher

NINJA FILE

LIKES: New lightweight shoulder armor

DISLIKES: Going it alone in the Never-Realm

FRIENDS: Akita

FOES: General Vex

SKILLS: Tracking and outdoors survival

GEAR: Katanas, oil lantern

KEY SET: Lloyd's Titan Mech

SET NUMBER: 70676

YEAR: 2019

Golden sword with a tassel is exclusive to Lloyd

Ninjago language "L" symbol on shoulder

LLOYD WITH A LAMP
In Lloyd's Journey (set 70671), the Green Ninja wears a black half-mask only instead of his usual hood. He fights with a flaming oil lantern while his gold sword is stuck in the ice.

LLOYD EMBARKS ON A SOLO QUEST in the frozen Never-Realm. Aspheera has blasted Zane out of Ninjago, and it is up to Lloyd to find him. Lloyd is equipped with a mech and weapons to deal with the local Blizzard Samurai. Hopefully his new ninja robes are suitable for cold weather!

AKITA
SHAPE-SHIFTING GUIDE

NINJA FILE

LIKES: Exploring
the outdoors
DISLIKES: People who
talk too much
FRIENDS: Lloyd, Kataru
FOES: Ice Emperor,
General Vex
SKILLS: Shapeshifting
GEAR: Dagger

KEY SET: Castle of
the Forsaken Emperor
SET NUMBER: 70678
YEAR: 2019

DID YOU KNOW?
Akita's twin brother
Kataru can transform into
a bear. The siblings found
their animal forms
in a Choosing
Ceremony.

Braided
hair design

Wolf symbol on
brooch clasp

Cape
resembles
tails

ANIMAL TRANSFORMATION
Formlings have the
power to shape-shift
into a particular
animal form. Akita
transforms into
a distinctive white
three-tailed wolf.
She first meets Lloyd
while in wolf form.

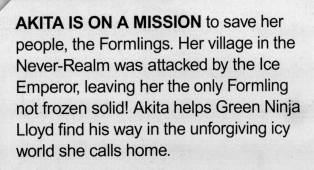

AKITA IS ON A MISSION to save her
people, the Formlings. Her village in the
Never-Realm was attacked by the Ice
Emperor, leaving her the only Formling
not frozen solid! Akita helps Green Ninja
Lloyd find his way in the unforgiving icy
world she calls home.

MASTER WU
ASPHEERA'S OLDEST ENEMY!

New head piece has more facial hair and a ponytail print on the back

New-look cape design is exclusive to Master Wu

Staff element appears in more than 800 LEGO® sets!

SHIP OF THE DESERT
Wu loves to take the wheel on the deck of the *Land Bounty*, the ninja's latest mobile base. A cross between the flying *Destiny's Bounty* and the six-wheeled DB X truck, it's ideal for fighting Pyro Vipers in the Desert of Doom!

NOW A FULLY GROWN ADULT AGAIN
(after a brief stint as a baby), Wu looks more masterful than ever in his broad new cape. He blames himself when Aspheera sends Zane to the Never-Realm, because he was the one who taught the snakelike sorcerer most of her Spinjitzu in the first place!

ICE EMPEROR

RULER OF THE NEVER-REALM

Face
distorted
by dark
powers

Scroll of
Forbidden
Spinjitzu
carried on
a naginata

Samurai-style
armor is studded
with ice crystals

ZANE REGAINED

The reign of the Ice Emperor
comes to an end when Lloyd
reminds him who he really is.
As soon as Zane is back to his
senses, he also gets back in his
ninja robes, which he wears to
pilot the Shuricopter (set 70673).

THIS FEARED RULER of the Never-
Realm is actually Zane, the Master of Ice.
He has been stranded far from home for
many decades and has forgotten his
friends. The dark influences of Forbidden
Spinjitzu and General Vex have turned this
brave ninja into a cold-hearted tyrant.

GENERAL VEX

PUTS THE ICE IN "NOT VERY NICE"

NINJA FILE

LIKES: Endless winter, bearing grudges
DISLIKES: Spring, summer, and fall
FRIENDS: Blizzard Samurai
FOES: The Formlings
SKILLS: Manipulation
GEAR: Ice spear, Ice Scroll of Forbidden Spinjitzu

KEY SET: Shuricopter
SET NUMBER: 70673
YEAR: 2019

Frozen mustache suits frosty features

A huge shard of ice cuts through Vex's armor, right where his heart should be!

ICE AND FIRE

As the true decision-maker behind the Ice Emperor's throne, Vex convinces Zane to create an Ice Castle and an enormous Elemental Dragon to guard it! Both appear in Castle of the Forsaken Emperor (set 70678).

Icicles hang from bottom of armor

DID YOU KNOW?

Vex was once a Formling like Akita, but he left the tribe when no animal joined with him in the Choosing Ceremony.

WHEN ZANE ARRIVES in the Never-Realm clutching the Ice Scroll of Forbidden Spinjitzu, Vex hatches a cruel plan. He makes Zane reboot so that he loses his memory, then convinces him to become the Ice Emperor—with Vex as his trusted advisor. Winter isn't the only thing in the Never-Realm that is bitter!

BLIZZARD SAMURAI
SNOWSTORM TROOPERS

NINJA FILE

NAME: Blizzard Archer
KEY SET: Castle of the Forsaken Emperor
SET NUMBER: 70678
YEAR: 2019

Ice is slowly covering this old soldier's armor

NINJA FILE

NAME: Blizzard Sword Master
KEY SET: Lloyd's Titan Mech
SET NUMBER: 70676
YEAR: 2019

Ice "horns" are built into Samurai helmet

Crossbow created for LEGO® Castle sets in the 1990s

Cool-blue katanas first seen in 2019

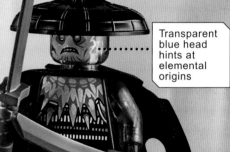

Transparent blue head hints at elemental origins

Armor covers a torso print also seen on the Blizzard Archer

NINJA FILE

NAME: Blizzard Warrior
KEY SET: Lloyd's Journey
SET NUMBER: 70671
YEAR: 2019

THE ICE EMPEROR has built up a large personal guard over the years. The Blizzard Warriors and Blizzard Archers lived as ordinary soldiers before the Emperor enslaved them, while the Blizzard Sword Masters are elemental beings, created using Forbidden Spinjitzu powers.

NYA FS
FORBIDDEN WATER MASTER

NINJA FILE

LIKES: Seeing Kai regain his powers
DISLIKES: Losing her water powers in a frozen Realm
FRIENDS: The FS ninja
FOES: Pyro Vipers
SKILLS: Forbidden Spinjitzu
GEAR: Katana, double-bladed dagger

KEY SET: Katana 4X4
SET NUMBER: 70675
YEAR: 2019

Ninja energy hoods made their debut in 2019

Double-bladed dagger is another new element

The Master of Water wears a stylized wave design

ONE GOOD TURN …
Each of the FS (Forbidden Spinjitzu) ninja can create an immensely powerful vortex around themselves. In set form, this is represented by a conical spinner with studs on the inside, allowing a minifigure to be securely attached and then spun into a blur!

SIMPLY TOUCHING THE Scrolls of Forbidden Spinjitzu can grant new and surprising powers. When the ninja make use of one of the scrolls, their Spinjitzu energy levels soar until they look like they're on fire! Nya's hood burns a watery blue when she unleashes her extreme new abilities.

JAY FS
FORBIDDEN LIGHTNING MASTER

Powered-up headwrap burns yellow like a fork of lightning

NINJA FILE

LIKES: Turning up the heat in the Never-Realm
DISLIKES: Burning through so many outfits
FRIENDS: The FS ninja
FOES: General Vex
SKILLS: Forbidden Spinjitzu
GEAR: Who needs gear in FS mode?

KEY SET: Shuricopter
SET NUMBER: 70673
YEAR: 2019

DID YOU KNOW?
The First Spinjitzu Master banned Forbidden Spinjitzu when he saw how it could warp a user's mind.

Outfit is mostly unchanged from Jay's standard 2019 robes

… DESERVES ANOTHER
When Jay activates his FS powers in combat with Vex, Zane plays his part in his ice-white Shuricopter. The flying machine has huge rotating shurikens on both sides, so Zane isn't left out of the spinning action!

Of all the FS ninja, only Jay's legs are a darker color than his top

JAY IS USED TO EARNING his skills through training and discipline, not getting them from a magical scroll! He knows that instant power without mastery or effort is a dangerous thing, and he must use the Scrolls of Forbidden Spinjitzu very carefully to keep himself from being corrupted.

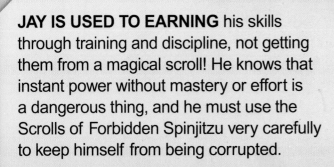

NINJA FILE

LIKES: Having new powers
DISLIKES: Knowing his new powers aren't earned
FRIENDS: FS ninja
FOES: Aspheera
SKILLS: Forbidden Spinjitzu
GEAR: Katana

KEY SET: Land Bounty
SET NUMBER: 70677
YEAR: 2019

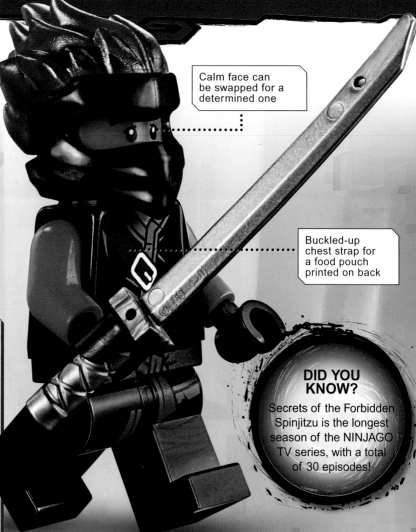

Calm face can be swapped for a determined one

Buckled-up chest strap for a food pouch printed on back

WHIPPING UP A STORM

The tornadolike spinner for each FS ninja minifigure is color-coded to that ninja's elemental color scheme. Each one is molded in two different colors, one of which is transparent with glitter elements inside it. Cole's spinner is black and sparkling transparent orange, matching his robes.

DID YOU KNOW?

Secrets of the Forbidden Spinjitzu is the longest season of the NINJAGO TV series, with a total of 30 episodes!

COLE BURNS BRIGHT when he uses the Scrolls of Forbidden Spinjitzu, and he must be careful not to let these new powers consume him! Even a level head like his can be turned by the promise of exciting new skills, and he must draw on his existing inner strength not to end up power-hungry like Aspheera.

NINJA FS

FORBIDDEN SPINJITZU MASTERS

Titanium metal face has a steely expression

Hotheaded Kai suits this look best of all!

NINJA FILE

NAME: Kai FS
KEY SET: Fire Fang
SET NUMBER: 70674
YEAR: 2019

Katana sword (just in case FS powers fail!)

Bright blue hands match belt printing

NINJA FILE

NAME: Zane FS
KEY SET: Lloyd's Titan Mech
SET NUMBER: 70676
YEAR: 2019

NINJA FILE

NAME: Lloyd FS
KEY SET: Castle of the Forsaken Emperor
SET NUMBER: 70678
YEAR: 2019

Lloyd's powered-up hood has an almost ghostly look!

Lloyd has mismatched arms

EVERY ONE OF THE NINJA is touched by the power of Forbidden Spinjitzu, but only Zane is briefly corrupted by it, owing to a bout of memory loss. Kai regains his stolen Fire Ninja skills without needing to use the Scrolls of Forbidden Spinjitzu at all, but he has since also harnessed his FS abilities.

SPINJITZU SLAM LLOYD
FORBIDDEN ENERGY MASTER TO THE MAX!

NINJA FILE

LIKES: Swords
DISLIKES: Spiders
FRIENDS: Slam stars Kai, Zane, and Jay
FOES: Uneven surfaces
SKILLS: Leaping into action
GEAR: Golden katana

KEY SET: Spinjitzu Slam—Lloyd
SET NUMBER: 70681
YEAR: 2019

Choice of powered-up or standard green eyes face prints

Lloyd wore his first golden hood way back in 2013

Waves of power are also printed on back

BACK WITH A SLAM
Spinjitzu Slam sets include a special FS ninja minifigure, a spinner, and a launcher to send the ninja spiraling into a range of targets. The buildable targets that come with Lloyd's set are three ice towers, each topped with a sword or a spider!

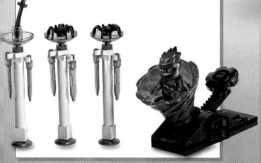

DID YOU KNOW?
Cole and Nya are the only two ninja minifigures not to appear in Spinjitzu Slam sets.

JUST WHEN YOU THOUGHT the ninja couldn't get more powered up, here comes Lloyd in his new Spinjitzu Slam gear! With Forbidden Spinjitzu energy surging across his entire upper body—not just his hood—he has the power to launch into the air and spin through any obstacles he encounters!

SPINJITZU SLAM NINJA

FS TORNADO TRIO!

NINJA FILE

NAME: Spinjitzu Slam Kai
KEY SET: Spinjitzu Slam—Kai vs. Samurai
SET NUMBER: 70684
YEAR: 2019

Golden glare can melt Blizzard Samurai opponents

Icy hood would give any other ninja brain freeze!

Same leg print as Kai's FS and standard 2019 minifigures

Standard face print on reverse of head

Outline of gi wrap still visible under energy pattern

Metallic arms match hood color

NINJA FILE

NAME: Spinjitzu Slam Zane
KEY SET: Spinjitzu Slam—Zane
SET NUMBER: 70683
YEAR: 2019

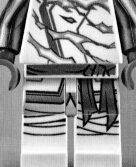

NINJA FILE

NAME: Spinjitzu Slam Jay
KEY SET: Spinjitzu Slam—Jay
SET NUMBER: 70682
YEAR: 2019

THE NINJA HAVE LEARNED to use their new FS energy powers for good in Spinjitzu Slam competitions. While Jay and Zane take on challenges with missile launchers and training dummies, Kai turns his tornado against a Blizzard Warrior to recapture the icy Scroll of Forbidden Spinjitzu.

CHAPTER TWELVE

NINJA VS. GAME MASTER

THIS ADVENTURE IS ON ANOTHER LEVEL!

IT'S ALL FUN AND GAMING when the ninja enter a virtual world called Prime Empire—right up until they realize they are running out of lives! Suddenly, the race is on to find three in-game Key-Tanas and defeat the ultimate end-of-level boss, Unagami!

DIGI JAY

HE'S IN THE GAME

Alternative face print shows a visor with a digital display

New shoulder armor won as an in-game upgrade

Circuit-style pathways crisscross the ninja's new robes

NINJA FILE

LIKES: Prime Empire
DISLIKES: Being trapped in Prime Empire
FRIENDS: Scott and Okino
FOES: Unagami
SKILLS: Stealth and dancing
GEAR: Katanas, flail

KEY SET: Jay's Cyber Dragon
SET NUMBER: 71711
YEAR: 2020

HAT BOX

Jay loves all the opportunities for dressing up in the Prime Empire. In Gamer's Market (set 71708), he can customize his look with a cowboy hat, a sailor's hat, and a top hat, as well as classic LEGO® Castle and LEGO® Space helmets!

DID YOU KNOW?

To escape the game world of Prime Empire, the ninja must collect a trio of "Key-Tanas"—part key, part katana!

JAY IS THE FIRST NINJA to play Prime Empire and the first to be drawn inside its digital world. After completing a series of fiendish quests, Jay is also the first to escape the game—and when he does, his upgraded ninja robes travel with him back to Ninjago City.

DIGI LLOYD

LEVELING UP

Digi-visor head turns to reveal Lloyd's usual green eyes

DID YOU KNOW?
Most inhabitants of Prime Empire are programmed "Non-Player Characters," also known as "NPCs."

Angular robe design suits an artificial gaming world

NINJA FILE

LIKES: Loot crates

DISLIKES: End-of-level bosses

FRIENDS: Digi ninja

FOES: Harumi NPC

SKILLS: Racing, inspiring NPCs

GEAR: Dao and katana swords

KEY SET: Jay and Lloyd's Velocity Racers

SET NUMBER: 71709

YEAR: 2020

RACING GREEN
To get their hands on one of three Key-Tanas, the ninja must win the Speedway Five-Billion road race. Lloyd's choice of vehicle for the race is a sleek green bike that leaves a trail of glowing energy behind it.

LLOYD, COLE, KAI, AND NYA follow Jay into the Prime Empire arcade game. They soon learn that Spinjitzu and elemental powers do not work there. Instead, they must build up their in-game stats to increase their strength and speed and earn credits to buy weapons and cool new digi-visor outfits!

NINJA FILE

NAME: Digi Kai
KET SET: Kai's Mech Jet
SET NUMBER: 71707
YEAR: 2020

Blades produced by game controllers are transparent

NINJA FILE

NAME: Digi Nya
KET SET: Jay's Cyber Dragon
SET NUMBER: 71711
YEAR: 2020

Health bar shows three lives remaining

Standard digi-weapons are not transparent

Swords and health bar slot into shoulder armor

NINJA FILE

NAME: Digi Cole
KET SET: Empire Temple of Madness
SET NUMBER: 71712
YEAR: 2020

Game controllers can project a range of weapons

Only Cole has digi-armor printing on his chest

AS PLAYERS IN PRIME EMPIRE, the ninja start out with four lives each. It may sound like a lot, but Prime Empire is a very dangerous place! A health bar displayed over each ninja's head shows how many lives they have left until it's well and truly game over.

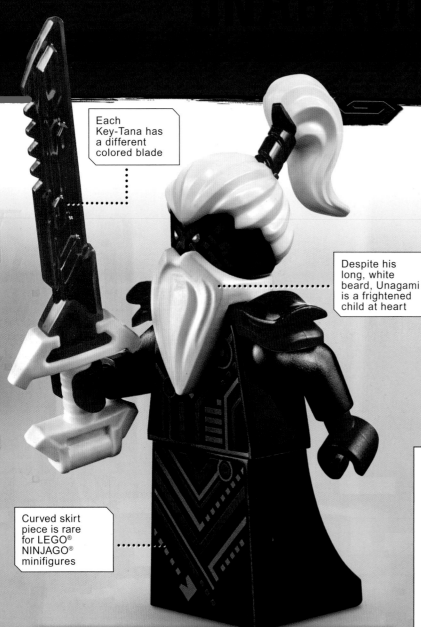

Each Key-Tana has a different colored blade

Despite his long, white beard, Unagami is a frightened child at heart

Curved skirt piece is rare for LEGO® NINJAGO® minifigures

NINJA FILE

LIKES: Turning players into energy cubes
DISLIKES: Disobedience
FRIENDS: Anyone who he can control
FOES: Rebellious players
SKILLS: Quick learner
GEAR: Digi-spear, Key-Tanas

KEY SET: Empire Dragon
SET NUMBER: 71713
YEAR: 2020

DRAGON DOWNLOAD
When Unagami gets really angry, he conjures up his Empire Dragon (or simply turns himself into it). The big, black beast has four clawed feet, two missile launchers on its shoulders, and a katana-sharp tail bringing up the rear!

PRIME EMPIRE STARTED OUT as a harmless arcade game, with the working title "Unagami" (short for Unfinished Adventure Game 1). But Unagami developed a mind of its own, becoming the angry ruler of his own playable world! Now Unagami wants to break out of the game and into Ninjago ….

RED VISOR

IN-GAME ENFORCER

404 is an online error code no gamer wants to see!

Visor obscures scary, fanged face

NINJA FILE

LIKES: Enforcing rules
DISLIKES: Obeying rules
FRIENDS: Flying drones
FOES: Rogue NPCs
SKILLS: Mobility and coordination
GEAR: Katanas, laser blasters

KEY SET: Ninja Tuner Car
SET NUMBER: 71710
YEAR: 2020

404

DID YOU KNOW?

Players who lose all their lives in Prime Empire become energy cubes to power Unagami's invasion of Ninjago.

MEAN CUISINE

The Red Visors may be Unagami's most visible attack force, but anything in his game world can become an enemy. In Empire Temple of Madness (set 71712), for example, the ninja have to battle flying, katana-wielding sushi!

Pixelated printing looks like data being destroyed

THE RED VISORS are Unagami's personal army, able to materialize anywhere in the game. Experienced NPCs know to stay out of their way, and the ninja soon learn to do the same. The Red Visors may not be smart, but they are relentless, and they don't always play by the rules!

AVATAR JAY

FAN FAVORITE

NINJA FILE

LIKES: Electric guitar solos
DISLIKES: Playing unplugged
FRIENDS: The League of Jays
FOES: Red Visors
SKILLS: Rocking out
GEAR: Prime controller, guitar

KEY SET: Jay Avatar—Arcade Pod
SET NUMBER: 71715
YEAR: 2020

Shiny, holographic stage makeup

Open jacket emblazoned with stars, studs, and lightning bolts

Ice-blue flesh for that zany spaceboy look

POD CASE

Each Arcade Pod set comes with two minifigures—a ninja in their Digi robes, and that same ninja's avatar identity. Both minifigures are stored inside a carry case shaped like a Prime Empire arcade machine!

DID YOU KNOW?

The Prime Empire arcade game is perfectly safe to play until you get to level 13. That's when it swallows you up!

JAY IS SO POPULAR that lots of Ninjago citizens play Prime Empire using Lightning Ninja avatars. So, to set himself apart in the game, Jay customizes his own look with a glam guitar-hero vibe. In his rockstar-inspired Avatar form, he shows the NPCs that they can be whoever they want to be!

AVATAR LLOYD

ALTERNATIVE LOOK

Avatar Lloyd shows off even more muscles than Avatar Jay!

Golden hair for the one-time Golden Ninja

First appearance of a baseball bat in a LEGO NINJAGO set

NINJA FILE

LIKES: Speedway Five-Billion racing
DISLIKES: Pre-programmed race results
FRIENDS: Mechanic Scott
FOES: Whack Rats
SKILLS: Blending in
GEAR: Prime controller, baseball bat

KEY SET: Lloyd Avatar—Arcade Pod
SET NUMBER: 71716
YEAR: 2020

DID YOU KNOW?

Prime Empire is made up of three main game zones—Terra Technica, Terra Karana, and Terra Domina.

BACKDOOR ACCESS

Each buildable Arcade Pod swings open on a hinge, just like the Prime Empire arcade machines in the NINJAGO TV show. The opening back wall has space to store a health bar, weaponry, and an avatar head.

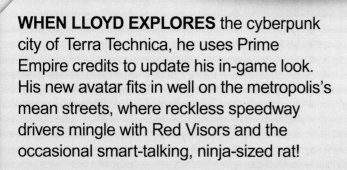

WHEN LLOYD EXPLORES the cyberpunk city of Terra Technica, he uses Prime Empire credits to update his in-game look. His new avatar fits in well on the metropolis's mean streets, where reckless speedway drivers mingle with Red Visors and the occasional smart-talking, ninja-sized rat!

AVATAR PINK ZANE

LAUNDRY MISHAP

NINJA FILE
....

LIKES: Being picked to play Prime Empire

DISLIKES: Costing 125 credits to unlock

FRIENDS: Other player avatars

FOES: In-game opponents

SKILLS: Player dependent

GEAR: Shurikens

KEY SET: Gamer's Market

SET NUMBER: 71708

YEAR: 2020

The eyes may look like Zane's, but any player can appear as this avatar

Original ninja mask mold made in pink for the first time

Pink robe design based on Zane's original white robes from 2011

IN THE PINK
Zane wears red-stained robes in one of the earliest episodes of the NINJAGO TV series, first shown in 2011. However, the pink version of the Ice Ninja did not become a minifigure at the time, making the 2020 version unique.

ZANE IS THE ONLY NINJA not to venture inside Prime Empire, owing to the risk that the game code could overwrite his Nindroid programming. However, a version of his look is available as a playable avatar in the game's marketplace—based on the time his white robes were washed with Kai's red ones!

AVATAR NINJA

PICK AND PLAY

Exaggerated fiery hairstyle is still recognizable in blond

Dynamite is Kai's arcade weapon of choice

A diver's mask hides Nya's face from passing Red Visors

Classic wetsuit is perfect for the Master of Water

NINJA FILE

NAME: Avatar Kai
KEY SET: Kai Avatar—Arcade Pod
SET NUMBER: 71714
YEAR: 2020

NINJA FILE

NAME: Avatar Cole
KEY SET: Gamer's Market
SET NUMBER: 71708
YEAR: 2020

NINJA FILE

NAME: Avatar Nya
KEY SET: Gamer's Market
SET NUMBER: 71708
YEAR: 2020

Avatar Cole's mustache is as bushy as his eyebrows!

Earth Ninja Cole digs the work-wear and pickax look

DESIGNING YOUR AVATAR in Prime Empire isn't just about looking different—it's about building a character you feel confident playing as. Kai, Cole, and Nya feel most confident as ninja, but they are willing to try out new looks when they have in-game credits to spare!

191

NINJA FILE

LIKES: Meditating
DISLIKES: Seeing Prime Empire players fail
FRIENDS: Past players
FOES: Unagami
SKILLS: Speed, agility, and patience
GEAR: Anything from his weapons stall

KEY SET: Gamer's Market
SET NUMBER: 71708
YEAR: 2020

Black hair tied up in the same way as Unagami's white locks

Shoulder bag for collecting credits

Silver dao blade from Okino's extensive armory

DID YOU KNOW?

During 2020, a real Prime Empire game could be played on LEGO.com —but no one ever got sucked inside it.

OKINO AND CO.

In the Gamer's Market, Okino runs an armory where Prime Empire players can buy colorful katanas and other samurai-style weapons. He is forever having to tell customers that the huge spinning blades above the shop are not for sale!

IT IS OKINO'S JOB to guide brave warriors through seemingly impossible Prime Empire challenges, making him one of the game's most important Non-Player Characters. He is shocked to learn that his whole existence has been part of a game, but the ninja show him how to live a life outside of his programming.

SCOTT

MYSTERIOUS MECHANIC

Dragon design continues on back of torso

Hat and hoodie are a single LEGO® element

DID YOU KNOW?

Prime Empire was created by game designer Milton Dyer. He stopped working on it when Scott disappeared.

NINJA FILE

LIKES: Improving things
DISLIKES: Taking unnecessary risks
FRIENDS: The ninja and the League of Jays
FOES: Red Visors
SKILLS: Finding and fixing design flaws
GEAR: Digi-scythe

KEY SET: Gamer's Market
SET NUMBER: 71708
YEAR: 2020

PRIME CANDIDATE

Scott was the first person ever to be drawn inside Prime Empire. As a young software tester, he gave the game its trial run and was never seen in Ninjago again!

SCOTT ONLY HAS ONE LIFE LEFT, so he has learned to be a cautious Prime Empire player. He repairs speedway cars for others rather than racing himself. He agrees to risk everything when he meets the ninja, however, as they show him how to take the fight to his old foe, Unagami.

AVATAR HARUMI

END-OF-LEVEL BOSS

This NPC has the same hair and makeup as the real Harumi

DID YOU KNOW?

Lloyd realizes this isn't the real Harumi when she doesn't remember the details of their first date together.

NINJA FILE

LIKES: Winning at all costs
DISLIKES: Not having the real Harumi's memories
FRIENDS: Unagami
FOES: Lloyd, her sole reason to exist
SKILLS: Impersonation, manipulation
GEAR: Katana

KEY SET: Gamer's Market
SET NUMBER: 71708
YEAR: 2020

MINIFIGURE MARKET

Avatar Harumi is one of many minifigures to feature in the 218-piece Gamer's Market set. This busy virtual market scene is one of the most crowded NINJAGO sets ever made, with nine minifigures.

Orange outfit has black stripes—a combination that often signals danger

THE REAL HARUMI is long gone, but she lives on in Lloyd's memory. Unagami takes advantage of this and creates a Non-Player Character who looks like Harumi to put the Green Ninja off his game. When this fake foe comes between Lloyd and the final Key-Tana, he has no choice but to fight her.

NPCS

NON-PLAYER CHARACTERS

Whack Rat head with built-in visor is one piece

Shoulder armor can hold katanas and a health bar

NINJA FILE

NAME: Sushimi
KEY SET: Empire Temple of Madness
SET NUMBER: 71712
YEAR: 2020

Pixelated cheese is an in-game reward

Sauce splotches on apron are blocky like old game graphics

NINJA FILE

NAME: Hausner
KEY SET: Jay and Lloyd's Velocity Racers
SET NUMBER: 71709
YEAR: 2020

NINJA FILE

NAME: Richie
KEY SET: Kai's Mech Jet
SET NUMBER: 71707
YEAR: 2020

Richie has a ponytail where Hausner has a horn

Outfit and in-game items are held together with tape!

THIS COLORFUL COLLECTION of NPCs are all in-game characters that Unagami relies on to do his dirty work. Sushimi is a chaotic, cleaver-throwing chef in the final Empire Temple of Madness level. The Whack Rats Richie and Hausner are street warriors who ride on rocket surfboards!

CHAPTER THIRTEEN

NINJA VS. SKULL SORCERER

IT'S TIME TO MOVE FROM LEVEL 13 TO CHAPTER 13!

ON THE SURFACE, the mountaintop City of Shintaro seems like a dream destination. But when the visiting ninja dig a little deeper, they discover the dark world of the Skull Sorcerer and his invincible Awakened Warriors!

HERO COLE
UNEARTHING MYSTERIES

NINJA FILE

LIKES: Making Mom proud
DISLIKES: Bottomless pits
FRIENDS: Princess Vania
FOES: The Skull Sorcerer and his Awakened Warriors
SKILLS: Teamwork
GEAR: Mace, shield, Swords of Deliverance

KEY SET: Skull Sorcerer's Dungeons
SET NUMBER: 71722
YEAR: 2020

Falling buffe armor instead of his usual ninja mask

New shoulder-guard also protects back

One arm left bare for maneuverability

LILLY OF THE MOUNTAIN
When Cole's mom, Lilly, visited Shintaro Mountain, she used the two Blades of Deliverance to defeat a marauding dragon. Now, these special swords have been stolen, and it is up to Cole and the ninja to find them!

Shadow Blade of Deliverance

DID YOU KNOW?
The Kingdom of Shintaro is a beautiful city on top of Shintaro Mountain. It is also known as the Ivory City.

IN THE KINGDOM OF SHINTARO, Cole dresses like a cross between a ninja and a knight. His heavy-duty armor is ideal for exploring the hidden cave system beneath the royal city. Only there can Cole unravel the mystery of his mother's time in Shintaro when she was the Master of Earth.

HERO WU
STILL ESSENTIAL

READY, PET, GROW!

The dragon that Wu rides in Shintaro was once Princess Vania's pet. Known as Chompy, the Shintaran Ridgeback started out small but soon grew too big even for grand royal apartments!

Spiky shoulder armor fends off foes— and parrots

Both Swords of Deliverance have skull-shaped pommels

Wu carries the Ivory Sword of Deliverance

AFTER MANY YEARS as their wisest friend and teacher, Wu is worried that the ninja do not need him anymore! In truth, they need him more than ever when they arrive in Shintaro. Wu's new look reflects the fresh sense of purpose he finds in the strange mountain kingdom.

HERO ZANE

A COLD KNIGHT IN SHINTARO

OH MINO OF MINE

Huge, hulking Minos are used as workhorses in Shintaro's secret mountain mines. Zane's Mino becomes his loyal steed, and he rides the rhinolike creature into battle against the Skull Sorcerer.

DID YOU KNOW?

While Wu and the ninja are in Shintaro, Misako and P.I.X.A.L. are keeping Ninjago City safe.

Golden lion shield matches Zane's new golden armor

Crossbow has appeared in more than 125 sets since 1990

NINJA FILE

LIKES: Seeing new places
DISLIKES: Being away from P.I.X.A.L.
FRIENDS: His mighty Mino
FOES: The Skull Sorcerer
SKILLS: Empathy
GEAR: Crossbow, shield

KEY SET: Zane's Mino Creature
SET NUMBER: 71719
YEAR: 2020

ZANE'S NEW ARMOR fits him perfectly, but that isn't true for everyone in Shintaro! When he meets a Mino—a monstrous mountain beast—he realizes that its bad temper is down to the uncomfortable armor it has been made to wear. When Zane frees the Mino, they become firm friends.

HERO NYA
QUEEN OF THE MUNCE!

Determined face can be swapped for a look of delight

Armor decoration looks like underground rivers

Fur provides comfort and warmth under armor

NINJA FILE

LIKES: Being a ninja
DISLIKES: Being a queen
FRIENDS: Wu, Jay, and the other ninja
FOES: The Skull Sorcerer and his Awakened Warriors
SKILLS: Dueling, peacemaking
GEAR: Spear and shield

KEY SET: Journey to the Skull Dungeons
SET NUMBER: 71717
YEAR: 2020

DID YOU KNOW?

At the same time that Nya becomes Queen of the Munce, Kai is elected to be leader of the Geckles!

ALL A BOARD

Set 71717 also doubles as a LEGO® NINJAGO® board game. Each move is decided by spinning a spinner—with Nya inside! Three other Shintaro sets work in the same way and can be combined to make one massive game.

UNDERNEATH SHINTARO CITY, Nya meets the troll-like Munce tribe and accidentally becomes their new queen! She doesn't really want the job, but she soon rises to the challenge. Thanks to Nya's inspiring leadership, the Munce unite with their old enemies, the purple, elflike Geckles.

HERO NINJA
NINJA IN SHINING ARMOR

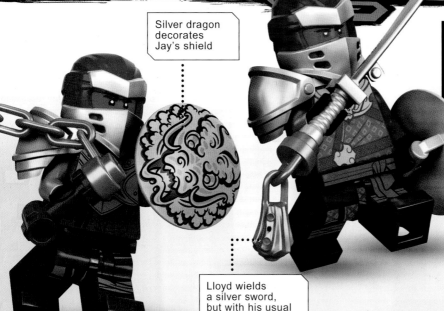

Silver dragon decorates Jay's shield

NINJA FILE

NAME: Hero Lloyd
KEY SET: Journey to the Skull Dungeons
SET NUMBER: 71717
YEAR: 2020

Lloyd wields a silver sword, but with his usual golden pommel

Rounded sword blade is a machete piece

NINJA FILE

NAME: Hero Jay
KEY SET: Journey to the Skull Dungeons
SET NUMBER: 71717
YEAR: 2020

NINJA FILE

NAME: Hero Kai
KEY SET: Fire Stone Mech
SET NUMBER: 71720
YEAR: 2020

Lion design marks Kai out as leader of the Geckles

THE COLOR OF the ninja's armor in Shintaro is determined by who they got it from. Jay and Lloyd wear silver suits made by the Munce, while Kai has golden gear created by the Geckles. The Munce have a silver dragon on their shields, while the Geckles go for a golden lion.

SKULL SORCERER
SHINTARO'S SPOOKY SECRET!

Mask lifts off to reveal the face of King Vangelis

This is the first NINJAGO minifigure with wings

Same lower body piece as Unagami, but with different printing

NINJA FILE

LIKES: Living in Shintaro
DISLIKES: The Munce and the Geckles
FRIENDS: The Awakened Warriors
FOES: Wu and the ninja
SKILLS: Sorcery and deception
GEAR: The Skull of Hazza D'Ur

KEY SET: Skull Sorcerer's Dungeons
SET NUMBER: 71722
YEAR: 2020

USING HIS HEAD
King Vangelis transforms into his winged form using the Skull of Hazza D'Ur. When he holds the ancient relic, he gains the powers of this long-gone dark sorcerer and can even animate dusty old skeletons!

SHINTARO SEEMS LIKE a perfect city, but its king, Vangelis, has a guilty secret. He lives a double life as the wicked Skull Sorcerer, who has enslaved the kingdom's underground tribes and made them dig for Vengestone. In this disguise, Vangelis wears a ghostly mask and flies on batlike wings!

DID YOU KNOW?

The distinctive heads of the Awakened Warriors were created in 2020 for these special new NINJAGO foes.

Helmet is reminiscent of retro Lord Garmadon

Green energy glows from inside the skull

All Awakened Warriors are identical

SKELETON CREW

The Awakened Warriors aren't the only beings to be revived by the Skull Sorcerer. Using the magical Skull of Hazza D'Ur, he has also reanimated the bones of Grief-Bringer, the huge dragon once defeated by Cole's mother.

NINJA FILE

LIKES: Obeying orders
DISLIKES: Being mistaken for Skulkin
FRIENDS: Other Awakened Warriors
FOES: The ninja
SKILLS: Pulling themselves together
GEAR: Vengestone spears

KEY SET: Skull Sorcerer's Dragon
SET NUMBER: 71721
YEAR: 2020

THE NINJA HAVE almost as much history with Skulkins as they do with snakes, but they've never seen anything like this before! Brought back to life by the Skull Sorcerer, Awakened Warriors can rebuild their bony bodies whenever a part breaks off them, making them almost invincible!

MURT
MANIPULATED MUNCE

Tall ponytail adds to Murt's imposing stature

Same style of armor worn by the Dragon Hunters

The Munce have green skin with blue markings

DID YOU KNOW?
The Munce like to confuse their enemies by curling into balls and rolling at their opponents' feet!

NINJA FILE

LIKES: Shiny things
DISLIKES: Thinking
FRIENDS: Other Munce
FOES: The Geckles
SKILLS: Digging and rolling
GEAR: Stone-breaking ax

KEY SET: Journey to the Skull Dungeons
SET NUMBER: 71717
YEAR: 2020

MUNCE AGAIN
Murt just might be related to his fellow Munce, Moe. Both look very similar, and Murt's shoulder armor is all that distinguishes them in Fire Stone Mech (set 71720).

LIKE ALL MUNCE, Murt has been tricked into thinking the Geckles are his enemy. His home is deep inside Shintaro Mountain, where his people once lived peacefully with the other tribe. Only when he meets the ninja does he learn that the Skull Sorcerer has been lying to both sides.

GLECK
GIFTED GECKLE

Working crossbow weapon fires LEGO® studs

Large, pointed ears make Geckles good listeners

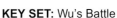
SWORD POINT
Most Geckles disagree with Gleck's positive opinion of the Munce. The sai-wielding Ginkle, for example, is convinced that the Munce stole the Geckles' Sword of Deliverance and should never be forgiven!

Short legs allow Geckles to access cramped caves and tunnels

DID YOU KNOW?
All Munce have names beginning with the letter "M," while the Geckles all have names that start with a "G."

GLECK IS ONE of the smartest Geckles and doesn't believe that his tribe of small purple people should be fighting the Munce. Years ago, he helped Cole's mother defeat the dragon that threatened Shintaro Mountain, and now he wants to help Cole in any way that he can.

PRINCESS VANIA
REBELLIOUS ROYAL

Vania is the first NINJAGO minifigure to wear this hair piece

Princess Vania's people all have pale skin and sharp cheekbones

BASE OF THE SKULL
The Skull Sorcerer runs his Vengestone mine from below the royal palace. Vania and the ninja must dodge its dungeons and brave its skull-shaped inner sanctum if they want to win.

NINJA FILE

LIKES: Dragons, reading
DISLIKES: Being told what to do
FRIENDS: The ninja
FOES: The Skull Sorcerer
SKILLS: Courageously following her own path
GEAR: Bow and arrow

KEY SET: Skull Sorcerer's Dungeons
SET NUMBER: 71722
YEAR: 2020

Cloud design on clothes suits Vania's mountaintop home

DID YOU KNOW?
Princess Vania is a big fan of the explorer Clutch Powers and often quotes lines from his books.

PRINCESS VANIA OFTEN DISAGREES with her father King Vangelis, but she is still surprised to find out he is the Skull Sorcerer! She is even more shocked when Vangelis banishes her to his Vengestone mine. Vania teams up with the ninja and helps them bring about a brighter, fairer future for Shintaro.

SPINJITZU BURST NINJA

NEW MOVES

Earth energy oozes out of Cole like lava

NINJA FILE

NAME: Spinjitzu Burst Lloyd
KEY SET: Spinjitzu Burst Lloyd
SET NUMBER: 70687
YEAR: 2020

NINJA FILE

NAME: Spinjitzu Burst Cole
KEY SET: Spinjitzu Burst Cole
SET NUMBER: 70685
YEAR: 2020

Lloyd's minifigure is made entirely from green parts for the first time

NINJA FILE

NAME: Spinjitzu Burst Kai
KEY SET: Spinjitzu Burst Kai
SET NUMBER: 70686
YEAR: 2020

COLE IS THE FIRST Elemental Master since his mother to unlock the Spinjitzu Burst move. The intense release of energy happens only if the user is surrounded by their element—just as Cole the Earth Ninja is inside Shintaro Mountain! The other ninja have since unlocked the power, too.

Luckily, the Fire Ninja's robes are flameproof!

ISLAND LLOYD

BACK TO NATURE

NINJA FILE

LIKES: Practicing bushcraft
DISLIKES: His mom going missing
FRIENDS: Nature!
FOES: The Keepers of the Amulet
SKILLS: Camouflage
GEAR: Katana, gold blade, dragon bone

KEY SET: Lloyd's Jungle Chopper Bike
SET NUMBER: 71745
YEAR: 2021

A dragon bone is a simple but effective weapon

Camouflage face paint made from mud and plants

Leaves in belt can be used for camouflage or food

DID YOU KNOW?
Misako and Master Wu set out to explore the island alongside the celebrity adventurer Clutch Powers.

SAND AND SURF

Lloyd's chopper bike is great for getting around the island. Its beach-buggy wheels are built for sandy and rocky terrain, and its top section separates for windsurfing on water—or in the sky!

WHEN WU AND MISAKO go missing on an unexplored island, Lloyd leads the ninja on a mission to find them. On the island, the other ninja are quickly captured by the same people holding Misako and Wu, but Lloyd is able to stay at large. He must adapt quickly and learn to live like a local!

ISLAND NYA
IN HER ELEMENT

Mask and armor add height to minifigure

Subtle, stylized wave design on torso

DID YOU KNOW?
Previous attempts to explore the island have been thwarted by strange and constant lightning storms.

Belt clip for connecting to climbing ropes

NINJA FILE

LIKES: Sailing away to parts unknown
DISLIKES: Not knowing where Master Wu is
FRIENDS: Zippy
FOES: The Keepers
SKILLS: Keeping an open mind
GEAR: Katana, double-bladed sword

KEY SET: Lloyd's Jungle Chopper Bike
SET NUMBER: 71745
YEAR: 2021

DEVOTED DRAGON
Nya's ocean-blue buddy comes to Lloyd and Zane's rescue in Jungle Dragon (set 71746). The creature is really very friendly—despite its fearsome-looking horns, teeth, and claws—and the ninja refer to it as Zippy.

AS THE MASTER OF WATER, Nya is central to the ninja's success on an island surrounded by ocean. While the rest of the team are on the lookout for a new enemy, Nya makes a new friend, in the form of a sea-colored dragon that will later come to their aid.

Sheathed katana for close combat only

NINJA FILE

NAME: Island Zane
KEY SET: Jungle Dragon
SET NUMBER: 71746
YEAR: 2021

NINJA FILE

NAME: Island Cole
KEY SET: The Keepers' Village
SET NUMBER: 71747
YEAR: 2021

Long-handled blade for hacking through undergrowth

Headband keeps hair and sweat out of eyes

NINJA FILE

NAME: Island Kai
KEY SET: The Keepers' Village
SET NUMBER: 71747
YEAR: 2021

Powerful Storm Amulet belongs to the islanders

Zane's belt is stocked with power packs

Gold machete blades

ALL SIX NINJA travel to the island, and each has a part to play in uncovering its secrets. Equipped with new tools and new-look outdoor wear, they find not only their missing friends—Misako and Wu—but also an isolated warrior tribe, dedicated to defending an ancient amulet!

ISLAND JAY
UNUSUALLY GIFTED

NINJA FILE

LIKES: Special treatment

DISLIKES: The thought of being eaten

FRIENDS: The Keepers of the Amulet (at first)

FOES: Anything that wants to eat him!

SKILLS: Looking on the bright side

GEAR: Katana, nunchaku blade

KEY SET: Catamaran Sea Battle
SET NUMBER: 71748
YEAR: 2021

Headband is molded into new-look hair piece

Utility belt holds water bottle

ALL AT SEA
When the Keepers are ready to feed Jay to Wojira, they speed him out to sea in a special cage-shaped boat. With no means of escape, he can only hope that the monster is just an island myth!

Extra utility pouch strapped around leg

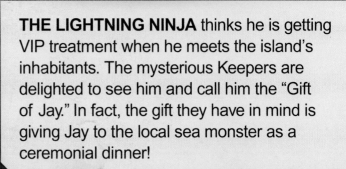

THE LIGHTNING NINJA thinks he is getting VIP treatment when he meets the island's inhabitants. The mysterious Keepers are delighted to see him and call him the "Gift of Jay." In fact, the gift they have in mind is giving Jay to the local sea monster as a ceremonial dinner!

CHIEF MAMMATUS

KING OF THE KEEPERS

Golden headdress passed down from chief to chief

BIG BROTHERS

As well as dragons and Keepers, the island is also home to living stone statues known as the Stone Golems. Created by the First Spinjitzu Master to help protect the Storm Amulet, these rock-hard guards cannot be stopped with elemental powers!

DID YOU KNOW?

According to Keeper tradition, no one who lays eyes on the Storm Amulet can be allowed to leave the island!

Ceremonial armor depicts the mighty sea serpent Wojira

NINJA FILE

LIKES: Statement headwear
DISLIKES: Brushing his teeth
FRIENDS: Poulerik
FOES: Outsiders
SKILLS: Leadership, loyalty
GEAR: Lightning staff

KEY SET: The Keepers' Village
SET NUMBER: 71747
YEAR: 2021

All the Keepers of the Amulet have lavender-colored skin

MAMMATUS IS THE LATEST in a long line of island leaders sworn to protect the Storm Amulet. This powerful artifact was given to his ancestors by the First Spinjitzu Master before Ninjago Island even existed. Like all Keepers of the Amulet, he tries to look as tough as possible to outsiders!

POULERIK

MAMMATUS'S HEAD MAN

Angry top head wears purple war paint

Lower, smiling head has white markings

Like most Keeper weapons, these sickles are made from wood and bone

HEAD TO HEAD
Two-faced PoulErik is well equipped to go head-on with a pair of ninja in the Jungle Dragon set. He keeps two of his eyes on Lloyd, who is riding the dragon, and the other pair on Zane, who is sailing a sky-skimming raft.

DID YOU KNOW?
Fangdam and Fangtom were the first two-headed NINJAGO® characters, but PoulErik is the first with two minifigure heads.

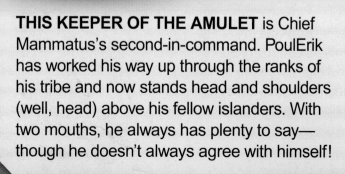

THIS KEEPER OF THE AMULET is Chief Mammatus's second-in-command. PoulErik has worked his way up through the ranks of his tribe and now stands head and shoulders (well, head) above his fellow islanders. With two mouths, he always has plenty to say—though he doesn't always agree with himself!

THUNDER KEEPER
COOKING UP A STORM

Mask patterns inspired by the look of the local dragons

Painted fangs only a slight exaggeration of real Keeper teeth!

DAYS OF THUNDER
In Jungle Dragon (set 71746), a Thunder Keeper tries to keep the Storm Amulet away from the ninja. The ancient artifact is usually kept in the Keepers' Village, where another Thunder Keeper guards his tribe's treasure from inside a cave.

DID YOU KNOW?
The special Storm Amulet piece is included in every one of the Island sets released in 2021.

NINJA FILE

LIKES: Lightning storms
DISLIKES: Clear skies and calm seas
FRIENDS: Other Thunder Keepers
FOES: Lightning Ninja
SKILLS: Conducting ceremonies
GEAR: Bone scythe, spear, and mask

KEY SET: The Keepers' Village
SET NUMBER: 71747
YEAR: 2021

Armor made from tree bark, vines, and thorns

BEHIND THIS FEARSOME MASK is an equally forbidding islander! He isn't in a bad mood though—he just takes his job very seriously. Using ancient chants and rituals, the Thunder Keepers call out to the storms that surround the island and asks them to never stop scaring off unwanted visitors!

RUMBLE KEEPER

A HUMBLE KEEPER

Shield with
sea-serpent
design

READY TO RUMBLE

A Rumble Keeper is just one of the foes faced by the ninja in Catamaran Sea Battle (set 71748). As the Keepers take to the water in lightning-powered craft, Kai sets sail in a flame-colored catamaran of his own!

Same clothing worn by Thunder Keepers and PoulErik

DID YOU KNOW?

In the NINJAGO TV series, greedy explorer Clutch Powers causes lots of trouble on the island!

RUMBLE KEEPERS ARE THE lowest-ranking Keepers of the Amulet, but their work on the island is still essential. As both guards and gardeners, they preserve the natural balance of their isolated home—sometimes tending to the flowers and other times fending off Clutch Powers!

IN 2021, LEGO® fans around the world celebrate the 10th anniversary of the LEGO® NINJAGO® theme. The LEGO Group marks the occasion in style, too—with some very special limited-edition minifigures that are dressed in head-to-toe gold!

TEN YEARS ON AND I DON'T LOOK A SINGLE DAY OLDER!

GOLDEN LEGACY KAI

ANNIVERSARY ARMOR

DID YOU KNOW?

Since 2011, more than 500 distinct NINJAGO minifigure designs and variants have appeared in sets!

Headwrap is a mold first seen in 2019 sets

Starburst shape is the Ninjago language symbol for the letter "K"

PLAY AND DISPLAY

Each 10th anniversary minifigure is found in just one 2021 set and comes with golden weapons, a buildable display stand, and a gold-colored tile printed with the "10 Years of NINJAGO" logo.

Each golden ninja wears the same hip sash and leg binders

WHO BETTER TO LIGHT THE CANDLES on a LEGO® NINJAGO® 10th birthday cake than the Master of Fire himself? Kai's flame-gold gear is the same color as his fellow anniversary minifigures, but with red accents and flame designs that are exclusive to him. He's really taken a shine to this look!

218

GOLDEN LEGACY LLOYD

ORIGINAL GOLDEN BOY

NINJAGO LEGACY
This special-edition Lloyd minifigure appears in the Legacy set Tournament of Elements (set 71735). The elaborate set is a fitting celebration of one of the ninja's greatest triumphs.

Hair with headband is a new piece for 2021

Inner layer of robes resembles dragon scales

Dragon-head design represents elemental energy

DID YOU KNOW?
Variants of the original Golden Ninja Lloyd had appeared in six sets before this anniversary minifigure was created.

LLOYD SETS THE BAR when it comes to gold-clad costumes. He was the first Golden Ninja in 2013, and back then he had a golden head as well! This anniversary minifigure is exclusive to just one 2021 set, in which Lloyd carries two golden katana swords—weapons he is very familiar with!

GOLDEN LEGACY NINJA

THE FULL TEAM

GOLDEN LEGACY JAY

Jay's golden hood has a Digi Ninja-style visor

Golden katanas match outfit

Hair with blue headband is a new piece for 2021

Lightning flashes decorate one side of Jay's robes

Wave pattern on robe and belt

LLOYD MAY HAVE BEEN the original Golden Ninja, but now everyone is getting in on the act! The rest of the ninja team all get to wear gilded gear during 2021 in special one-off set appearances. How will the heroes top the look for their 20th birthday in 2031?

GOLDEN LEGACY NYA

GOLDEN LEGACY NINJA
THE FULL TEAM

Master Wu is the only anniversary minifigure with a golden face

First time Wu's beard piece has been made in gold

An Earth-splitting hammer is Cole's signature weapon

Zane wears FS energy hood in gold, rather than white

Zane doubles up on metallic detail with his titanium face decoration

GOLDEN LEGACY WU

Cole's helmet is the reverse colors of the version worn in 2020 by Hero Cole

Inner Nindroid workings are exposed

GOLDEN LEGACY ZANE

Golden armor as worn on adventures in Shintaro

Pattern on upper belt is different for each ninja

GOLDEN LEGACY COLE

CHARACTER INDEX

Acidicus 26
Acronix 118
Akita 171
Arkade 159
Aspheera 165
Awakened Warrior 203
Bansha 89
Blizzard Archer 175
Blizzard Sword Master 175
Blizzard Warrior 175
Bolobo 69
Bonezai 17
Bytar 33
Captain Soto 113
Char 166
Chew Toy 159
Chief Mammatus 213
Chokun 33
Chope'rai 74
Chopov 16
Chopper Maroon 142
Claire 99
Clancee 102
Clouse 71
Cole
  Airjitzu Cole 93
  Armor Cole 169
  Avatar Cole 191
  Cole 6
  Cole DX 19
  Cole FS 178
  Cole ZX 22
  Deepstone Cole 85
  Digi Cole 185
  Dragon Master Cole 163
  Fusion Cole 127
  Ghost Cole 108
  Golden Legacy Cole 221
  Hero Cole 197
  Hunted Cole 153
  Island Cole 211
  Jungle Cole 77
  Kimono Cole 41
  NRG Cole 35
  Resistance Cole 134
  Spinjitzu Burst Cole 207
  Spinjitzu Master Cole 149
  Techno Cole 51
  Tournament Cole 63
Commander Blunck 120
Commander Raggmunk 121
Cowler 91
Cyren 105
Cyrus Borg 50
Daddy No Legs 157
Dareth 97
Dogshank 104
Doubloon 105
Echo Zane 110
Eyezor 72
Fang-Suei 29
Fangdam 29

Fangtom 28
Flintlocke 103
Frakjaw 17
Garmadon
  Emperor Garmadon 145
  Lord Garmadon 11, 44
  Master Garmadon 49
General Cryptor 56
General Kozu 46
General Machia 117
General Vex 174
Ghoultar 89
Giant Stone Warrior 113
Gleck 205
Golden Ninja see Lloyd
Gravis 69
Green Ninja see Lloyd
Griffin Turner 68
Harumi
  Avatar Harumi 194
  The Quiet One 137
  Princess Harumi 136
Hausner 195
Heavy Metal 156
Hutchins 138
Ice Emperor see Zane
Iron Baron 155
Jacob 69
Jay
  Airjitzu Jay 93
  Armor Jay 169
  Avatar Jay 188
  Deepstone Jay 82
  Destiny Jay 106
  Digi Jay 183
  Dragon Master Jay 162
  Fusion Jay 127
  Golden Legacy Jay 220
  Hero Jay 201
  Hunted Jay 153
  Island Jay 212
  Jay 8
  Jay DX 19
  Jay FS 177
  Jay ZX 23
  Jungle Jay 77
  Kimono Jay 40
  NRG Jay 35
  Resistance Jay 135
  Spinjitzu Master Jay 148
  Spinjitzu Slam Jay 181
  Techno Jay 53
  Tournament Jay 64
Jesper 98
Jet Jack 158
Kai
  Airjitzu Kai 92
  Armor Kai 168
  Avatar Kai 191
  Deepstone Kai 83
  Destiny Kai 109
  Digi Kai 185

Dragon Master Kai 163
Fusion Kai 124
Golden Legacy Kai 218
Hero Kai 201
Hunted Kai 153
Island Kai 211
Jungle Kai 76
Kai 7
Kai DX 18
Kai FS 179
Kai ZX 23
Kimono Kai 39
NRG Kai 35
Resistance Kai 135
Spinjitzu Burst Kai 207
Spinjitzu Master Kai 146
Spinjitzu Slam Kai 181
Techno Kai 52
Tournament Kai 62
Kapau'rai 75
Karlof 67
Killow 141
Krait 73
Krazi 17
Kruncha 13
Krux 119
Lasha 27
Lizaru 27
Lloyd
  Armor Lloyd 170
  Avatar Lloyd 189
  Deepstone Lloyd 80
  Destiny Lloyd 109
  Digi Lloyd 184
  Evil Green Ninja 81
  Fusion Lloyd 126
  Golden Legacy Lloyd 219
  Golden Ninja 43
  Green Ninja 37
  Hero Lloyd 201
  Hunted Lloyd 151
  Island Lloyd 209
  Jungle Lloyd 77
  Lloyd FS 179
  Lloyd Garmadon 21
  Resistance Lloyd 131
  Spinjitzu Burst Lloyd 207
  Spinjitzu Master Lloyd 149
  Spinjitzu Slam Lloyd 180
  Techno Lloyd 53
  Tournament Lloyd 65
Lord Garmadon see Garmadon
Luke Cunningham 143
Master Chen 59
Master Wu see Wu
Master Yang 114
Maya 129
Mezmo 31
Mindroid 57
Ming 90
Misako 95
Morro 79

Mr. E 139
Murt 204
Nadakhan 101
Nails 143
Nindroid Drone 57
Nindroid Warrior 57
Ninjago Mailman 96
Nuckal 15
Nya
  Armor Nya 169
  Avatar Nya 191
  Deepstone Nya 87
  Destiny Nya 107
  Digi Nya 185
  Fusion Nya 125
  Golden Legacy Nya 220
  Hero Nya 200
  Hunted Nya 152
  Island Nya 210
  Nya 10
  Nya FS 176
  Resistance Nya 135
  Spinjitzu Master Nya 147
  see also Samurai X
Okino 192
Overlord 45
P.I.X.A.L. 55
  see also Samurai X
PoulErik 214
Princess Vania 206
Prison Guard 113
Pyro Destroyer 167
Pyro Slayer 167
Pyro Whipper 167
Pythor
  Pythor 60
  Pythor P. Chumsworth 25
The Quiet One see Harumi
Rattla 31
Ray 128
Red Visor 187
Richie 195
Rivett 122
Ronin 86
Rumble Keeper 216
Samukai 12
Samurai X
  Jungle Samurai X 66
  P.I.X.A.L. Samurai X 133
  Samurai X 36
Scott 193
Skales 30
Skalidor 32
Skip Vicious 143
Skull Sorcerer 202
Skullbreaker 159
Skylor
  Hunted Skylor 144
  Skylor 61
Slackjaw 123
Sleven 73
Slithraa 31

Snake Jaguar see Zane
Snappa 29
Snike 33
Soul Archer 88
Spitta 27
Spyder 91
Sqiffy 105
Stone Scout 47
Stone Swordsman 47
Stone Warrior 47
Sushimi 195
Tai-D 111
Tannin 123
Thunder Keeper 215
Ultra Violet 140
Unagami 186
Vermin 123
Wail 91
Wrayth 89
Wu
  Dragon Master Wu 161
  Golden Legacy Wu 221
  Hero Wu 198
  Master Wu 5, 24, 172
  Techno Wu 54
  Teen Wu 160
  Temple Wu 94
Wyplash 14

Yang's Student 115
Zane
  Airjitzu Zane 93
  Avatar Pink Zane 190
  Deepstone Zane 84
  Destiny Zane 109
  Dragon Master Zane 163
  Fusion Zane 127
  Golden Legacy Zane 221
  Hero Zane 199
  Hunted Zane 154
  Ice Emperor 173
  Island Zane 211
  Kimono Zane 42
  NRG Zane 34
  Prisoner Zane 112
  Snake Jaguar 132
  Spinjitzu Master Zane 149
  Spinjitzu Slam Zane 181
  Techno Zane 53
  Titanium Zane 70
  Zane 9
  Zane DX 19
  Zane FS 179
  Zane ZX 23
Zugu 73

DK | Penguin Random House

Project Editor Beth Davies
Senior Art Editor Anna Formanek
Managing Editor Paula Regan
Managing Art Editor Jo Connor
Production Editor Siu Yin Chan
Production Controller Lloyd Robertson
Publisher Julie Ferris
Art Director Lisa Lanzarini
Publishing Director Mark Searle

Designed for DK by Lisa Sodeau.
Additional minifigures photographed by Gary Ombler.

DK would like to thank Randi K. Sørensen, Heidi K. Jensen, Paul Hansford, Martin
Leighton Lindhardt, Tommy Kalmar, Morten Rygaard Johansen, and Michael Svane
Knap at the LEGO Group. Thanks also to Rosie Peet, Nicole Reynolds, and
Lisa Stock at DK for editorial assistance and Kayla Dugger for proofreading.

MIX
Paper from
responsible sources
FSC™ C018179

This book was made with Forest
Stewardship Council ™ certified
paper – one small step in DK's
commitment to a sustainable future.
For more information go to
www.dk.com/our-green-pledge